Routledge Revivals

The Economic Consequences of Power Production

First published in 1931, *The Economic Consequences of Power Production* presents an analysis of the societal and economic impacts of the increasing reliance on electricity and mechanized power. The book, written by Fred Henderson (1867-1957), has been part of early 20th century discourse about automation, productivity, and work-life balance. It is noted for its critical perspective on the potential negative consequences of unchecked technological advancement, as suggested by a 1933 New York Times review that described it as offering "A Gloomy View of Power Age Consequences." This work remains an important historical reference for scholars interested in the history of technology and its societal impacts.

The Economic Consequences of Power Production

Fred Henderson

Routledge
Taylor & Francis Group
ROUTLEDGE REVIVALS

First published in 1931
by George Allen & Unwin Ltd.

This edition first published in 2025 by Routledge
4 Park Square, Milton Park, Abingdon, Oxon, OX14 4RN

and by Routledge
605 Third Avenue, New York, NY 10158

Routledge is an imprint of the Taylor & Francis Group, an informa business

A Library of Congress record exists under ISBN [if unavailable then LCCN]:

ISBN: 978-1-041-16426-5 (hbk)
ISBN: 978-1-003-68456-5 (ebk)
ISBN: 978-1-041-16430-2 (pbk)

Book DOI 10.4324/9781003684565

THE ECONOMIC CONSEQUENCES OF POWER PRODUCTION

by

FRED HENDERSON

LONDON
GEORGE ALLEN & UNWIN LTD
MUSEUM STREET

FIRST PUBLISHED IN 1931
SECOND IMPRESSION 1932

PRINTED IN GREAT BRITAIN BY
UNWIN BROTHERS LTD., WOKING

THE ECONOMIC CONSEQUENCES OF POWER PRODUCTION

CHAPTER I

The vast enlargement of our powers of production by the application of science to the processes of the world's work has for the most part been discussed as if all the questions arising in connection with it were questions relating to effectiveness in production only. The purpose of this book is to call attention to certain aspects of it of basic importance in relation to the distribution of the wealth so copiously produced by these modern methods—a line of enquiry which I hope to show leads to a somewhat clearer understanding of the urgent problems now confronting us in our industrial life than we seem so far to have reached. In regard to unemployment, for example, the pretty complete failure of all Governments—prolific in sure remedies when out of office, and with the utmost good will and intention sterile in results when given the opportunity—is, I think we shall find, in large measure because the significance of this direct and vital relation of our modern methods of production to distribution as well as to production itself has been so generally missed.

Our urgent problems in politics and economics are with regard to distribution. So far as production is concerned, our capacity is so great that practically any demand for goods could be met without delay or difficulty if economic conditions permitted. Vast power, continuously expanding to vaster power, has been brought under control and is visibly up to its job if it gets its chance. The difficulties of our productive system are not in the defectiveness of its own powers. They are difficulties thrust upon it by the irregularities and confusions of the world's markets; and in so far as it works confusedly, irregularly, and much below its own capacity, that is because it receives its orders from the consuming side of the world's economy, and is governed by the distribution of purchasing power and effective consuming demand. No suggestion of its own incapacity arises; so far as that is concerned it stands confidently and efficiently ready to do whatever may be demanded of it.

In marked contrast with this productive efficiency, our distribution of purchasing power is inadequate, confused, and without any sort of intelligent adjustment to the needs of human life and the ability of production to serve those needs to the full. Trade depressions, in which abundant real wealth plainly required for the satisfactions of life cannot be marketed, and further production is shut down because no corresponding purchasing power has been distributed, are constant reminders to us of this contrast between our power for effective production and our failure in distribution. In a world of abundant resources, and at a period in history when those resources have risen to a level beyond the dreams of any previous generation, masses of the population in all countries are for some reason restricted in consumption to the poverty level of a world of scarcity and a period of famine; and quite obviously that reason is not the inability of our producing powers to meet their needs. There is in all this a very urgent call to every one of us for the most searching and earnest scrutiny of our distributive methods; with a view to discovering the causes of so grotesque a maladjustment between what our productive capacity has made possible for us and what our present methods of getting it distributed allow to pass on into use and consumption. Somewhere in the process the natural flow of the world's resources into the world's life is being held up; and a sufficiently searching scrutiny of the economic channels through which we direct their flow should reveal where and why the constriction takes place.

My purpose here is to offer for such scrutiny the proposition:

> That the maladjustment is due to our failure to diagnose accurately the real character and significance of the change which science has made in our methods of production:
>
> that the fundamental change so made demands certain corresponding changes in the economy of distribution:
>
> that our distributive system, in its essential character, remains on a pre-science age basis, wholly unadjusted to the change; its economics the obsolete economics of a handicraft age of production, inapplicable to the new processes:
>
> and that our failure to adjust it to the new facts in production is the explanation of its incompetence

to fulfil the proper function of a distributive system, which is to ensure the passing on of products to their intended use and consumption without impediment or limit up to the full capacity of production to provide them for the needs of the world's life.

CHAPTER II

In inviting such a scrutiny, my first duty is to set out with clearness and precision the basis of my case in regard to what I have alleged to be "our failure to diagnose accurately the real character of the change which science has made in our methods of production." There is, of course, no claim to be made to the discovery and presentment of facts hitherto unknown. All the facts in such a matter as this are well known. It is with their significance and character, with their dynamic interpretation in relation to the economics of distribution, that this scrutiny is concerned.

When we wish to sum up the character of this period of modern scientific production, the almost invariable way of doing so is to define it as "the machine age." What apparently everybody sees as the central factor in it is the machine; and to the machine is attributed all the vast increase in our productive power and all the change which has been wrought in the conditions of life.

But is that a really penetrative definition? Is the machine anything more than the vehicle for the really operative factor in the great change which has taken place? Is it not in terms of power and energy rather than of mechanism that the true character of the industrial revolution must be stated if its full significance is to be grasped? Here at the outset, it seems to me, the general use of such a phrase to describe the period of modern industry warrants a suspicion of error in the generally accepted view of what the industrial revolution means; at any rate a suspicion of wrong emphasis and a missing of the relative importance of things. Quite literally, it puts the cart before the horse; gives priority of significance to the thing which is moved over the power which moves it.

For, if you will think of it for only a moment, the most complicated and wonderful machine in the world is in itself as passive and inert as any heap of pebbles on the roadside. It is designed and put together with amazing skill; part adjusted to part to receive and convey and transform motion to a given end in the shaping of materials into products. But it remains a thing inert in itself; a thing which does not move unless and until it is moved and kept in motion by the continuous impact of power upon it; a receptacle and a channel for power. The really fundamental thing we have to consider is the energizing of the machine; the nature of the powers and not the ingenious construction of the mechanism by which those powers are harnessed for their work.

As a receptacle in which power can be so trapped as to confine its effort to escape to certain designed channels and the making of the precise impacts which do our work for us, modern machinery is an amazingly ingenious thing; so amazing that it is hardly to be wondered at if people, seeing it in movement, should think of the machine almost as a thing with an activity of its own, and forget that it does nothing but move as applied power drives it, in the directions and the relation of parts for which its construction provides. But for all that there is nothing essentially new, nothing to bring about a revolutionary change in industry, in mechanism as mechanism. It is the secondary and sequential thing in the application of science to production. The knowledge of power which can be set to work is the primary and originating thing. Given that, and the making of mechanical devices for directing its work to such ends as we may set for it is a matter of skilful adjustments rather than of origination, however marvellous such devices may be in their contrivance. Man has always been a tool-using animal within the limit of his knowledge of power by which the tool could be operated. The primary and defining fact about the modern application of science to industrial processes is, I repeat, not the mechanism but the energy employed.

The new thing, the really fundamental thing, the profoundly important thing which defines the industrial revolution, is the substitution of other powers for human physical effort as the working energy of the world's production.

Man's ability to secure or produce more or less wealth for the satisfaction of his wants and desires has always depended upon his possession and use of adequate tools. He only began to emerge into a life that could be called even primitively civilized as such aids to his activities began to be devised and used. The original hunter's power in the pursuit of food was multiplied many times over by his bow and arrow and other weapons. The man who sets out to compel the soil to yield him food, if he tries to cultivate his garden with his bare hands will make no job of it at all; equipped with spade and hoe, his productive capacity increases by an almost incalculable multiplication from the practical zero of his own unaided power. In the making and devising of tools, man has been extraordinarily ingenious; but always he has been limited in respect of such tools by his knowledge of power by which they could be operated; and until yesterday practically the only power within his knowledge was the power of his own muscles.

If you could transport yourself backward in history some two hundred years and watch the people of that day at their work, you would find them producing wealth slowly and on a small scale; with an equipment of simple tools only, the hammer and the saw, the spade and the reaping-hook, of which the defining and limiting characteristic was that they were tools within the capacity of a man's arm to operate. Varied and ingenious as man's tool-devising has been, to that limit his lack of knowledge of other powers has always confined him; and his tools until this age have always been extensions of the human hand and the physical powers of the human body. That has been the governing factor in all his working devices.

The fact that from the earliest days he has possessed some slight knowledge of other powers enabling him to devise a few machines differing in this essential character from his ordinary tools constitutes no real departure from this general human limitation. Long before the age of modern power-production, he devised waterwheels to use the power of running water and windmills to harness the power of the moving air to the task of grinding his corn. Greatest of all his achievements in this direction was his compulsion of the winds to carry him about the seas of the world in sailing-ships. All these things were in a degree true machines in the modern sense; traps to catch power other than his own physical strength and make it work for him; tools that differed not merely in degree but in essential character from his ordinary ingenious devices for making his own bodily energies more effective. But they were applied only to a fractional part of his work; and in one quite vital respect these slight approaches to a knowledge in some degree comparable with the knowledge of power which has made the modern machine possible fell hopelessly short. He could only use these other forces when he found them manifesting themselves in Nature on their own account. He could not command their presence at his will when and where he wanted them. When the wind died down or the stream ran low, his sails hung motionless, his ships lay becalmed and helpless, his wheels stopped turning. He could set his little trap across the track of this or that natural energy, and by waiting until it moved of its own accord along its own paths he could borrow from it the movement which he wanted. But such casual and dependent use of a power which happens to be disporting itself regardless of human intentions is not the mastery of power on which modern industry has been created. To generate, to make energy appear and work at his bidding at his own chosen time and place, only when science taught Man that secret was power dependably enslaved to human uses with the real mastery on which a system of production could be founded for the assured and regular service of the daily needs of human life. It was a slight and imperfect knowledge of power, and in its imperfection was applied to so proportionately small a part of the general activities of life as not to affect in any general way the limitation set by his own bodily powers to man's tool-devising.

As for his extensive use of the strength of other animals, it was too closely akin to his use of his own muscles to make it a new sort of knowledge of power or a real departure in kind from his limitations. It enabled him to devise tools a little heavier and productive of more results; but they were tools identical in character with those he himself used in hauling and carriage and such other tasks as animals could be set to. The difference was quantitative only, not qualitative; a difference between a larger and a smaller waggon, a heavier and a lighter load; but nothing in this use of animals carried his conception of power beyond the idea of living muscular effort; a little more capable of sustained endurance than his own, but identical in kind.

None of these marginal things affect the truth of the generalization that for all the substantial purposes of his life and work Man's tools for immemorial generations were only an extension of the muscular power of living bodies, and were energized only by that power; multiplying his productive capacity many times over, but all within the narrow limitation of bodily strength and endurance in setting and keeping the tool in motion. To that limit was our productive power confined in all history until our own time; and what science has given us to-day is not merely more production but a new kind of production, a new character to the work of the world.

CHAPTER III

The general view of the modern machine, the view which, even when not directly expressed, is implicit in practically every discussion about it, is that it is the latest advance of mankind in what has from the earliest times been the continuous improvement of our working instruments, a development in direct and unbroken line of our human craft in implement making; in a word, that it is the old tool become larger, more effective, more complex. Brief as has been the scrutiny of the facts up to this point, it is sufficient to show that this view is erroneous. The modern power-machine is a new thing; it is the embodiment of a profound and vital change in the relationship of human labour to the processes and products of the world's work. So far from being a development in direct line of improvement upon our old implements, its appearance makes a revolutionary breach in the continuity of our working methods and in the very nature of the effort by which Man turns the raw resources of the world he inhabits into sustenance for his life and usable satisfactions for his needs and desires.

In so far as the new powers with their appropriate machines are used in production, their purpose and effect is to make human labour obsolete as the physical energy of production; the exact reverse of the purpose of the old tool, which was to make human labour more effective in functioning as the physical energy of production. The blow given with the old handicraft hammer was given by the physical energy of the arm wielding the hammer. All the force of it was the force put into it by human muscles. What the hammer provided was an extension of the arm into a hard striking surface instead of a fist of soft flesh which could not without injury deliver the impact with the full force which the arm was capable of putting into it, with an added leverage to the arm itself in multiplication of that force. But the hammer-stroke was the arm-stroke; human labour functioning as the sole driving and energizing force of the process. The stroke of a steam-hammer is another thing altogether. It is not human physical energy better and more forcibly applied, as the purpose of the old tool was to enable it to be, but the superseding of human physical energy by other and vaster driving and propellent powers.

It is in this respect that the term "labour-saving" as applied to the modern machine has a significance much deeper than general usage gives to it; a meaning quite distinct from the same term as it might have been applied to the old tool. For the old tool also had a labour-quantitative effect. Working with good tools, well-adjusted and proportioned, meant the expenditure of fewer hours of labour in securing a given product than working with poor tools; and a general improvement and better adjustment of tools meant the need for fewer men for a given output. But it was the same sort of labour applied to production in essentially the same way as before, whether the tool was primitive or improved; labour more efficiently applied by reason of the improvement in the tool, but unchanged in the qualitative character of the human physical energy by which the whole process was activated. And with that restriction upon the development of the tool—the impossibility of making anything more of it than was permitted by the strength of the human hand by which it had to be grasped and operated—its labour-quantitative effect in reducing the number of men required for a given output was also kept within narrow bounds.

The vital and qualitative sense in which the power-driven machine is "labour-saving" is that the human service associated with the machine has ceased in its essential character to be labour in the old sense. It is not only a matter of dispensing with a certain number of men, but of dispensing with a certain function of labour. What is required from the fewer men is something which differs absolutely in character from what had previously been the labour factor in production; and the key to it is the disappearance of the power-supply function of labour, the supersession of the physical energies of men's bodies by other non-human energies as the driving-force to which the tool responds. This, as we shall see, is something much more than a quantitative difference. Not only is its final result in the displacement of men in relation to output on another scale altogether from the displacement effected by any betterment of the old hand-driven tool, but in its repercussions on the economic life of the world, and its effect upon our distributive system in particular, so different a thing as to need a world of new economic relationships to adjust it to the human needs it might serve so superbly and now serves so ill for lack of such gearing.

The point can best be made clear if we turn for a little from these generalizations about it, and examine a modern plant of power-machinery in operation; and at this stage in the presentment of my case I will ask you to come with me for a tour round the electricity generating works of which I have the honour to be a director. The machines are very wonderful; but we will, if you please, concentrate our attention upon the men, noting the detail of their work with a view to defining the character of the human service required in relation to the machine throughout the whole process, from its beginning with the arrival of the coal to the final point at which the cables leave the works carrying the generated current to a great population for domestic and industrial use as light and heat and power.

From the top of the main building there emerges into the open air, through an open archway some fifty feet up, a telpher track which runs, supported on lattice steel pillars, in manifold curves over the considerable open space adjoining the works. This open space has a navigable river on one side and a railway depot on the other; and you will see part of the works' coal supply lying in barges at the wharf, and part brought in trucks by rail; the telpher track running over all. There is one man in the telpher cabin; and we will go inside the works and up to the top and watch him. We find, on stepping out of the lift which takes us up, that the archway through which the telpher runs in and out is the open end of a long alley-way extending right across the interior of the building, and that the floor of this alley is a series of coal bunkers over which the telpher track is continued inwards. The one man in the telpher cabin is the only man here. He runs his engine out, stops when over the barge which is being unloaded, lets down the open grab, which closes on its ton of coal, raises the load, travels with it back again inside the building—pausing for a moment at the entrance, when the load is automatically weighed and registered in passing—and opens the grab to deposit its burden in the bunker most needing replenishment. What he does during the two minutes of raising this ton from the barge to the bunker at the top of the building is to touch the appropriate switch or button or lever at the appropriate moment, releasing or shutting off power; with an expenditure of his own physical energy in the process that would not lift a pound of coal three feet.

In these days of almost universal motor-driving, most people will be familiar with the character of such work as this, and what qualities are needed for it. Everyone who gets a motor-car and within a week or so finds himself out on the roads with it, knows that in the first place it is a matter of understanding the movement and effect of a few simple controls, and after that the growth of experienced confidence and familiarity in handling them. Pretty well all the labour required in the ordinary working of power machines is of this character. Discretion, judgment—the ordinary qualities of sound intelligence—with accuracy of timing and of touch, these are required of our man in the telpher cabin; but physical human force as the energy of any part of the process not at all. One other man co-operates with him, the man in the barge or the truck at the ground level; who, at the moment when the grab is suspended over the coal, ensures by a touch as it swings easily at the end of its supporting cable that it descends at the right spot. At the finish of the unloading there is a slight call for the old labour factor; for the grab does not clean up all the fragments, and a few shovels full remain to be trimmed out by hand labour. Both that and the guidance of the descending grab are, however, eliminated when coal coming in trucks is automatically tipped into a collective pit for the telpher grab to work upon.

Here then, we have our coal deposited in the upper bunkers; and from that point onwards no human service whatever is needed in connexion with it. These bunkers are huge funnels, immediately over the boiler-house, and are narrowed at their lower ends to pipe-shoots by which the coal is delivered by gravitation to the furnaces in the quantity and at the rate required. The delivery is made into a trough which runs across the front of the furnace at the level of the furnace-bed. This bed is not a fixed grate, but a revolving carrier band which moves slowly from front to back inside the furnace, returning again underneath. The coal, deposited by gravitation in the trough, falls on to this moving furnace-bed through a regulated shutter opening on the inner side of the trough, and this slit, extending across the whole width of the furnace front, is widened or narrowed according to the load required. The fuel is carried slowly and evenly through the furnace, combustion being complete by the time it reaches the further end, where the downward revolution of the carrier tips the clinker out at the back into a water-filled trough about two feet deep. This trough runs to the outer wall of the building, and at the bottom of it a carrier surfaced with catch compartments takes the clinker, which is cooled in passage, to the end of the trough, out of which the carrier then rises in an incline and passes through a wall opening to a raised platform outside the building, where it tips its load into a funnel bunker from which the clinker is automatically loaded for removal into lorries underneath.

From the moment the coal arrives at the works till the lorry is driven away with the refuse, at no point in any of the movements or processes through which it passes does human labour provide any power-supply whatever for the movement. Nobody touches or handles it. The armies of sweating men who used to work to scorched exhaustion shovelling coal through furnace doors have all vanished. In their place are two men attached to each boiler furnace. Conservatism in nomenclature still persists absurdly in calling them "stokers"; but anything in the way of actual stoking is quite extinct in the service they give. They are, in fact, combustion engineers, whose job is to see to it that the furnace does its work without a hitch and according to the pressure required. This they do by watching a panel on which some half-dozen dials automatically register the various pressures and rates of movement which need to be kept under constant supervision, and by making the necessary adjustments according to the tale told by the dials; adjustments which, as in the case of the man in the telpher cabin, mean turning off or increasing the supply or the direction of power by touching the appropriate switch or lever in the appropriate degree.

The temperature in these furnaces to which the nest of tubes constituting the boiler is exposed is from two to three thousand degrees, and the purpose of all the work so far as we have followed it up to this point is to produce a head of dried steam at a pressure of about 250 lb. to the square inch. But before following that tremendous energy up to the work it is generated to perform, we may as well finish with the furnaces themselves, and see what sort of human service is required in dealing with the loaded fumes they give off; for the subsidiary mechanism of flues and means of dealing with furnace fumes might be expected to give rise to some demand for human physical force as the energy of the process of cleaning. You will, however, find as little of it there as elsewhere. The fumes are cleaned of their heavy impurities by centrifugal mechanism in great closed chambers and the resultant debris is removed by vacuum suction. A basement vacuum-cleaning installation is connected by tube to all the necessary flue points.

The steam goes direct from the boiler-house to the great machines in which the electricity is generated. As my purpose here is not technical, but only to observe the character of the human service associated with the machines, I need not enter into any detailed description of these great and fascinating turbine generators. It is sufficient to say that the whole machine is constructed for the reception of this high-pressure steam by a system of turbines so as to enable it to perform the task of rotating a huge steel cylinder which runs down the centre of the actual generating chamber in the interior of the machine. This cylinder is magnetized and inset with certain copper parts. Round it at the requisite distance are copper coils; and its rotation produces the electric current by induction in these coils.

Two men only are required in attendance on this mammoth £50,000 power-machine. Getting the machine up to its full speed is a matter of about ten minutes at starting; opening the steam valve, starting the oil pump, and regulating the controls by adjustments to the gradual rise in speed until the machine is running all out. None of these operations involve more than small movements of the valve handles and the various levers of control. The human service required is solely concerned with the regulated admission and direction of power to the machine; and the acts of admission and direction are, generally speaking, the slightest touches on controls making no appreciable call for physical effort. The only operation inclined to be heavy is the turning of the steam-valve handle, and that can be done by touching the button of a little electric motor geared to the valve handle for the purpose.

Once started, the service which the machine requires from the men in charge is that of constant examination, watching oil gauges and the like, and moving the appropriate control if and when any need for adjustment reveals itself to their constant scrutiny. The oiling is automatic, except that one or two grease-cups at outlying small-friction points not reached by the automatic oiling system may require to be filled once a day. The speed of the machine is kept automatically regular by a centrifugal speed governor. The human labour factor associated with the machine is constant supervision and watchfulness and readiness to adjust the controls of the power-service as required.

The generated current passes out from this department by cables to the various feeders going off in all directions from the works to the consumers. In the switch-board room clock-index-faces register the pressure with which the current is coming off from the turbine generators and passing into the various feeders and mains; and the essential character of the human service here is precisely the same constant watchfulness and readiness as in the other stages of the work. The one place in the works where you will find some requirement for human labour as the physical energy of a process is in repairing. The heavier repairing tools, lathes and drills and the like, are power-driven machine tools; but a certain amount of hand tool work is also necessary, and physical labour in the lifting and movement of materials under repair. It is only at these outer fringes of the work, and quite apart from the main operations of the undertaking, that a minute survival of the old labour factor as power in a process can be discovered at all.

CHAPTER IV

This example which I have taken at some length and in considerable detail does not represent the all-round development of our power-machine effectiveness over the whole range of manufacture. I have chosen it purposely for that very reason. It marks about the furthest point of attainment, and therefore reveals with greater clearness and simplicity the character of the labour change which is implicit in the power-driven machine. It shows, in a practically completed development, the end to which every improvement in power-driven machinery brings us nearer. It is in the nature of things that the change should be carried furthest most rapidly in industries whose product is an intangible thing like electric power than in industries engaged in shaping tangible commodities from raw material which has to be grappled with at every stage in the manufacturing process. The advance of power-machine production has not therefore been an even advance over manufacturing industry as a whole. It goes on rapidly here and slowly there, for reasons which we will examine in a moment; and you will find every stage of the development, from still surviving handicraft processes up to the practically complete disappearance of the power-supply function of labour as in the case we have examined, still present in our methods of production. But over the whole field the change goes on without ceasing; at the handicraft end it is more and more only in the odd corners and interstices of production that the older function of labour is to be discovered; and where it does survive it is no longer taken to be normal or permanent. The points at which a demand for human labour as a power-supply still remains are regarded only as temporary imperfections in the power-system, gaps to be filled in. Research and invention fasten incessantly upon every such hiatus in the system; and there is hardly a day in which some such gap is not finally closed up—in the tiny detail of a process here and in a major operation there—absorbing into the power system yet another surviving remnant of the old labour system.

The degree and the rapidity with which this goes on depend on many things; on the character of the raw material, on the simplicity or complexity of the finished commodity, and whether it is an assembly of many separate parts like a boot or a simple and uniform thing of one material and texture throughout like a screw, and yet again in the case of composite finished commodities on the similarity or variableness of the parts which have to be assembled. Compare, for example, the complexity of joining the upper of a shoe to the sole with the simplicity of pressing a prepared deal into the groove prepared for it in another deal as part of the power-machine process of making doors and window-frames in modern building-trade joinery.

The difficulties of changing an industry over from the labour-power-supply basis to the power-machine system are at their maximum when they are difficulties in all these particulars together; a raw material refractory to mass handling, a complex finished commodity of many parts, and a variability between the parts themselves making their assembly an intricate process. Having examined the simple case of electric generation at one end of the wide range of power-machine development, it will perhaps help to an understanding of the general facts if we examine the case of an industry which is quite at the other extreme in respect of complexity and difficulty; and the production of boots and shoes is probably the most instructive example.

Here you begin with a raw material most intractable for machine purposes. The distinction between material which is conformable and material which is refractory to mass shaping by power-machines is, generally speaking, the distinction between made and natural raw material. Compare, for example, the boot and shoe trade with leather as its raw material and the clothing trade with its raw material in woven fabrics. The woven fabric is even and regular in texture and thickness, uniform throughout. You can put a compressed bale of it under a cutting machine adjusted to the necessary pattern, and with one movement of the machine cut out a stack of identical parts of identical mass-produced garments. But no two hides of leather are alike. They vary in thickness, texture and quality; not only as between one and another, but as between parts of the same hide, which has to be selectively scrutinized over its whole surface. From the tanning process to which it has been subjected it comes to the boot factory a prepared raw material; but in its essential grain and texture it remains a natural product, with all the inequalities, local blemishes, and variability of a natural product. Hence the initial stage in the production of boots has, up to the present, remained for the most part the work of the individual clicker cutting out single parts to his standard pattern and exercising careful selection on his raw material. And following upon that initial difficulty is the multiplication of parts, and the further difficulty of assembly created by their many variations in pliability, thickness, and treatment required on assembly. So great are these difficulties that the making of boots was quite one of the latest of our productive activities to come into the factory system. Until very recently it remained a scattered home industry carried on by individual handicraft; such workshops as were provided for congregated work were handicraft workshops in which the raw materials were cut out to pattern, and the parts so prepared were, within the working experience of all but the younger generation still employed in the trade, given out to be lasted and stitched and riveted into boots by home workers with nothing but the primitive equipment of the old cobbler in their own kitchens.

In a present-day power-plant boot factory a pair of boots or shoes passes through from two to three hundred separate processes between the first handling of the hides to the final trimming and boxing of the finished article in readiness for distribution to the retailer and the public. One long set of processes deals with the uppers and another with the soles, converging to the point at which they are put together and the boot as a whole becomes subject to a further long series of operations. To follow a pair of shoes through these hundreds of processes from start to finish is to see pretty well every stage in the history of power-machine development. Here and there an operation remains entirely handicraft. In others the machine is simply a moving knife or a boring or stitching or pulling-over instrument, sometimes hardly developed at all from the old handicraft tool, sometimes much more complex; but whether simple or complex, having the common characteristic that instead of a hand-driven tool being applied to the material as in the old days, the tool is now power-driven and the material has to be hand-served to it. Along the line of processes through which the shoe passes, at first in separate parts and later in assembly, this type of machine will be found in great variety in regard to the degree of skill which it demands from the worker associated with it. In some operations the feeding of material to the machine is quite simple and unskilled, in others a very high degree, indeed, of skill and expertness is needed; and almost every gradation between these two extremes is represented at some point or other in the variety of processes. Not many of these machines are yet developed to the point of gripping the material—the partially made boot or separate part at the stage of the particular process—and giving it the movement necessary to enable the machine to operate upon it as required at that stage. The workman in charge of the more complicated processes has to guide the material with great exactness through its evolutions of presentment to the operative point of the machine, with a precision and often a delicacy of touch and a strained attention much greater than when he had both tool and material in his own hands. Then, as handicraftsman, he had to adjust two movements both under his own control—his grip on the material and his action with the tool—whereas now the tool is in rapid independent movement, rotating or shuttling at a pace to which he must keep the exactest time and the most precise degree of pressure and movement in his manipulation of the material.

There are other operations in which the machine has been developed beyond this stage; processes in which the machine itself grips the material and moves it with precision through the required operation. But these are rare as yet. The difficulties which we noted at the outset are so great that in the main the machinery of the industry is still largely in the half-and-half stage at which, while human physical energy has been eliminated as the power-supply for the action of the tool, the incapacity of the machine to deal automatically with a refractory material and a complex assembly of parts still leaves a great deal of the power-supply on that side of the operation to be provided by the human worker; and often with a degree of skill and strained concentration all the greater because of the pace set for him by the power-driven capacity of the machine to pass a greatly multiplied volume of work through any given process in any given time. When, in addition to the character of the original material, it is remembered that the raw material for any one of this long series of operations is the separate part or the assembled boot at the stage to which all the previous operations have taken it, the difficulties in the way of complete automatism in the machine and the elimination of contributory skilled human-energy participation in such operations will be apparent.

Here, at any rate, in the most difficult type of industry for power-machine purposes, so difficult that the machine was wholly excluded from it for a long time after other great industries had been completely transferred to the power system, the advance has been rapid once the beginning was made. In what degree and how quickly the power-machine will take possession of the remaining ground as yet beyond its capacity, or whether it will ever wholly occupy it, is a matter of interesting speculation. But if the record of the past ten years, and particularly the past two or three years, in the introduction of new boot and shoe machinery is any index to what will yet be achieved, it is certain that the development will be great; and that if a proportion of human work as the power and skill of certain operations as well as their supervision is likely to remain essential in such an industry, it will be very considerably reduced from what it is to-day. Quite recently the pace of the development in this direction has been greatly accelerated. The results are not yet fully manifest in any British boot and shoe factory so far as I know; but elsewhere they are very manifest indeed. At the moment, the end of 1930, the output per worker employed in British boot and shoe production is 20 pairs per week. But in America it has risen to 35 pairs, and in the biggest and most up-to-date manufactory in Europe, the Bata establishment in Czechoslovakia, it is 40 pairs per week; not in the least because of any incapacity on the part of British workers, but because of the more effective methods in use elsewhere. The British industry keeps going for the time against this intensive competition largely by specializing, outside the ordinary production for general wear, on certain styles and fashions to which the intensified methods are not altogether applicable.

The question of competition between the more and the less completely equipped units of production in different parts of the world is, however, outside my purpose, which has solely to do with the development of the machine from the point of view of its effectiveness in dispensing with the power-supply function of labour. Our concern in this enquiry is with the basic power now being made available for the industry anywhere, and not merely the immediate competitive equipment of trade rivals. The main line on which this rapid advance has been made, especially in Czechoslovakia, is the organisation of work on the separate parts, which are much simpler to deal with and more amenable to power-machine treatment, so as to reduce to the lowest possible minimum the number of operations afterwards required in the assembly workshops, where the difficulties of automatism in the machine are greatest; and having so reduced them, to deal with them in the assembly shops by the conveyor method, with its team of co-ordinated workers to each conveyor unit; a method which, I believe, has not up to the present been adopted in any British factory.

The final test of all this, the measure of the effectiveness with which the difficulties in the way of the power-machine are being overcome in an industry peculiarly unsuited to its development, is the great reduction of labour costs per unit of the completed commodity. Up till three or four years ago the entire factory working costs, including wages and overheads, had never anywhere been lower than 30 per cent of the whole cost of the finished article, as against 70 per cent for raw material costs. And that was regarded as a great achievement, a most exceptional degree of efficiency. These relative averages were, and still are in many factories, more in the neighbourhood of 35 and 65 per cent. To-day, raw material costs in the Bata establishment are 80 per cent, and labour costs only 20 per cent. All this development has been within some three or four years; and shows how swiftly the human service required for the passage of any given volume of raw material through all the processes of manufacture is decreasing. The decrease is, in fact, greater than these figures would indicate, for they are figures of cost, and in each year during the period to which they refer individual wages have been higher.

CHAPTER V

I know of no manufacturing industry in which the development of the power-machine towards automatism and the elimination of the power-supply function from the human service associated with it is so difficult as in the boot and shoe industry. I have taken it purposely as the most backward in this development, just as I took the electric generation industry purposely as the most advanced; firstly in order to show how great the development is and how rapidly it is proceeding even in the most backward example one can find; and secondly because its difficulties in such an industry throw a useful light upon the factors by which the development of the power-machine is conditioned, and so enable us to get a clearer comprehensive view of the stage to which the industrial revolution has advanced over the general field of our productive activities.

Generally speaking, the raw material handled by our great industries is produced so as to be as conformable as possible to automatic handling by the power-machine. There is but a slight proportion of the world's manufacturing activities in which natural material with its natural flaws and obstinacies and irregularities has to be used, and our power processes restricted to meet its unavoidable difficulties. Over nearly the whole range of production, raw material is turned out in the suitably prepared condition for easy mass handling by power-processes, and its preparation from the crude natural state into an industrial raw material presents no difficulty. Metals and textiles constitute the great bulk of raw materials in the general volume of the world's manufactures; everything else lumped together is little more than marginal. And metals and textiles are prepared—and lend themselves to such preparation without any obstruction due to the character of the crude natural ores and growths from which they are prepared—so as to be completely conformable to power-machine operation. The manufactures dependent upon them were almost as far advanced towards automatism as electric generation now is, long before a difficult and untypical industry like shoemaking had started on the road at all. The essentially simple operation which we began by examining—the operation of regulating the admission of power with the requisite pressures into the chambers of a machine prepared and channelled to receive and direct it, within which it does the whole work of production out of sight and out of touch, the product being a product of the movement of the machine under the impacts of the admitted power, with no raw material complications—may be taken in the main as representing the final stages in the industrial revolution, from which most of the textile and engineering trades now fall but very little short. Allowing for the necessary difference made by a tangible raw material and a tangible commodity, they come practically into the same category. All their one-piece processes and simpler combinations are power-machine automatism from start to finish; and in such production as finally involves a more intricate assembly of parts, rationalization in the lay-out and sequence of the assembly work, with the conveyor as the factor for making sequence effective by scientifically timed and co-ordinated team work, is the potent agent in reducing to a steadily decreasing minimum such human service other than supervision for which the necessity still survives. Wood probably bulks next largely after metals and textiles among the raw materials of the world's industry; and for most purposes of common usage is as conformable to power-machine handling. Amongst the newer materials rubber figures largely, and is also conformable. Leather is an outstanding exception. And over the whole range, including the exceptions in respect of refractoriness, the record everywhere is a record of less and less labour in relation to the unit of output; more and more raw material shaped into final products for each hour of human labour associated with the process; more and more produced wealth with less and less human time and energy consumed by and embodied in each unit of it.

Except for what is now only a small and still dwindling margin of our activities in drawing and shaping from its natural sources the wealth which sustains and equips human life, production has escaped from the limitations of human physical energy. The energy which, in various forms of power, moves and handles and shapes those natural resources into commodities for human use and convenience, is a vaster thing altogether, and the implements devised for it to work with enable it to pour out at our bidding products in such abundance as mankind heretofore has only been able to imagine in fables of the enslavement of genie who could build a palace in a night at their master's word. We to-day have Aladdin's lamp in our hands. We have enslaved the elemental powers of Nature to our service; and our human labour is a matter of rubbing the lamp and ordering the slave of the lamp to perform miracles of work for us. The function of labour is now to admit the power to the machine, to regulate its degree and direction according to the stage in a process and the particular impress which is to be made on the raw material at that stage; the function of manipulating power controls.

The general necessary productive labour of the world tends more and more to a uniformity of this machine-minding type. The qualities and characteristics of this type demand a little close study; for it is a new thing; as new a thing in human activity as the power-machine is amongst implements. Its advent as the new and general type of labour is the necessary adaptation of human effort to the requirements of the power-machine. It is labour on a perceptibly higher level of general intelligence than the labour which was classed as unskilled in the old manual processes; and nearly always it has a greater strain of responsibility imposed upon it than was the case with any of the unskilled labour associated with handicraft. But it is intelligence and responsibility which has nothing in common with what has hitherto been known as skill in craftsmanship.

The men employed in a shoe factory are still called shoemakers; but there is no such thing as a craftsmanship of shoemaking in the work of the mass of the men so employed. There are a few managing men at the centre, surveying and dealing with the work of the factory in its entirety, to whom it is a shoe factory in which their duties are related to the craft of shoemaking; and the under-managers and foremen of particular sections of the work covering a series of processes have something of the same craftsman's view of their duties as appertaining to shoemaking. But for the mass of the workers attending this or that machine which performs this or that one of the two or three hundred separate processes in the making of a shoe, they might just as well be working in a tobacco factory or at steel-pen making or any of scores of other occupations for anything of shoemaking craftsmanship there is in their particular job. They are machine-minders of the type now common to all power-machine industries.

I may best illustrate the point by returning to my previous instance of the almost universal motor-driving habit we have developed in these days. Nobody will suggest that driving a motor-car or motor-cycle is unintelligent work. It calls for a general intelligence and alertness and a quick sense of responsibility. But when we speak of skilled and unskilled workmen, these are not the qualities on which the distinction is made. The basis of the distinction between skilled and unskilled in industry is knowledge and craftsmanship in relation to a particular trade; its special tools and the handling of them; its material and the technique of dealing with it under all conditions; knowledge and craftsmanship not to be acquired except by long, specialized training. In that sense, driving a motor is obviously not a skilled activity. A few days' possession of a car or cycle gives to any ordinary intelligent person a knowledge of its power-controls and how they act; and in a week or two one is running about the roads in and out of other traffic with a growing confidence. The feel of the steering-wheel becomes familiar, the response to emergencies becomes automatic; and all quite readily to anyone of ordinary intelligence without any preliminaries of long training and technical study. The skilled workman in handicraft was responsible for a complete result in which the whole process was dependent upon his personal exercise of power over tools and materials, and every movement was the co-ordinated movement of his own hand with the guiding intention of his own mind directing it. The human labour associated with the modern power-machine, of which motor-driving is the most familiar example, has nothing to do with the actual work performed, but only with switching on or switching off the operative non-human powers which perform it. The human skill and alertness are concentrated on the power-controls and stop short at that.

That is precisely the sort of intelligence and understanding called for in what now tends to be the general and uniform type of machine-minding labour; not the energizing of any process, with all it involves by way of intimate knowledge of the tools used and the materials wrought upon and the relation of every energizing movement to the needs of a finished product; but simple readiness, expertness, and a dependable degree of judgment in attending to the machine-controls so that the power which does energize it can do its work most smoothly and efficiently. During the war you would have seen in almost any munition engineering workshop the most oddly assorted collection of workers—clergymen, young girls a month or two after school leaving, all sorts of volunteers who had never handled machines before—attending to complicated mechanism with intelligence and efficiency; precisely the same sort of intelligent efficiency with which the stream of motor-cars and cycles on any busy highway is directed on its course by a similar miscellaneous crowd of drivers.

In that sense, production has not only escaped from the limitations of human physical energy, but also, as far as the general mass of workers are concerned, from the limitations of specialized and highly trained technical human skill. The new powers do their work for the most part without requiring for their ordinary supervision and control more than the common intelligence of the ordinary man or woman; and the special skill, the intimate knowledge of the industry in relation to its material and its completed product, which used to be the necessary equipment of every handicraft worker, is highly concentrated in a small central staff of experts.

This follows naturally and inevitably from the disappearance of the power-supply function of labour in production. With that disappearance there necessarily disappears also all that we have hitherto known as skill in craftsmanship. Such classifications of labour are the classifications of a handicraft age. The skill of craftsmanship is in the personal application of personal energy to material which has to be studied closely and known intimately in all its characteristics and resistances when wrought upon; the effect of different tools upon it and the methods of applying them so as to subdue its resistances; its amenability to this or that mode of treatment; and the variation of treatment necessary under varying conditions. Think, for example, of the carpenter's equipment of tools to meet the widely differing resistances of his material to treatment; cross-cutting and with the grain, surface smoothing, boring, grooving, and the score of other problems presented to the wood-worker in the application of the right tool in the skilled way to the varied conditions of handling and shaping his material. All such skill in craftsmanship resolves itself into supplying the precise energy in the precise direction requisite for the purposeful shaping of the material at every stage in the progress of the work in hand, with a finished commodity in mind all through, to which every detail of the work is related.

Eliminate the power-supply function of labour, and all this is eliminated with it. The human service associated with the power-machine ceases to be labour in the old sense with the cessation of this primary function of labour and all that it carried with it in the old world of human activity in production. The old intimacy with material and with a particular craft and a particular product vanishes just in proportion as the power-machine becomes the sole energizing factor in each process of production; and the new type of machine-minding labour, manipulating a few simple power-controls, emerges as the common type for all power-machine industries. The new type has to conform to the requirements of the new conditions in intelligence, alertness and activity; but these qualities demanded from it are no longer related to a craft or a product, but to the movement of the machine. And in the most important matter of all from the point of view of this enquiry, the function of this new type of labour has ceased to be a factor in the measurement of output. That is determined by the degree of power which the machine can be constructed to carry, and the extent to which the machine can transform power pressure into the requisite effective movements. Output in production has escaped from the limitations of human physical energy.

On the other hand, as we have seen, the craft knowledge which is finally embodied in the completed product, knowledge of materials and their qualities, and of the relation of all parts to the whole—knowledge which was the necessary equipment of every handicraft worker—has now become the specialized function of small central staffs of managing experts and technicians. But the character of this human service also has been transformed out of all recognition from what it was when it was one strand woven into the general necessary equipment of the handicraft worker. Every handicraft worker had to possess this knowledge of the craft in relation to its material and its product because, in his capacity as the power-supply factor in production, he had to guide his hand and tool by it in the manipulation of his material, and make an operative effectiveness of it at every stage of the work. His mind and his physical energy worked together indivisibly, his trained hand with the rightly selected tool doing the bidding of his informed will in a single movement of intelligent human workmanship; and this movement, in which physical energy and skill and general craft knowledge were all combined, was the complete service of production. From its raw condition to its final form, the material which was wrought into a finished product had this service and this only spent upon it; a complete service of many qualities, all compact in the single craftsman.

These qualities and functions have now become entirely separate. The energy has become non-human. The skill with which the energy is applied to the shaping of the material has also become non-human, a matter of precisely designed mechanism responding to the impact of power so as to cut or mould or join the material with an exactness which the most experienced human hand with the most intelligently applied craft knowledge moving and directing it could rarely or never achieve. And this craft knowledge—the mind and understanding behind the hand and the physical energy—this also has been largely separated from its old operative function, and has become in the engineer and the chemist and the technician a function of study and research by which to determine the effective relation of the power to the machine and of the machine to the material; a function in production wholly different from the continuous application of his craft knowledge by the craftsman to every movement of his hand and every moment's guidance of his tools.

The handicraftsman has, as it were, been split up into three parts. The physical energy which he contributed to production has been superseded by the new gigantic powers: his operative skill has been superseded by the precision of mechanism: and his craft knowledge has become the technician's specialized knowledge of the reactions between these non-human factors and the materials of his particular industry. Thus the craftsman completely disappears; and what the power-machine industry requires by way of labour is an altogether new function for which there was no counterpart quality in the handicraftsman at all. The mass of the workers called into existence by the new conditions as machine-minders are an entirely new type; concerned neither with the technique of materials nor with the productive purpose of the machine in relation to a finished commodity, but only with the movement of the machine as a thing in itself; and with that movement only at second-hand; not by effecting it directly, but by attending to the controls which admit and regulate the effective power. And what that means by way of creating a new general type of human service in relation to power-production can best be described by citing an example; as when Mr. A. S. Pearse, in his *Cotton Industry of Japan and China* (1929), points out that progress in mechanical inventions has made skill so unimportant that Japanese girls from the rural districts are able to compete in all the requirements of the industry, so far as the general mass of human service in it is concerned, with British and European operatives of however long experience.

CHAPTER VI

For the purposes of our enquiry, the outstanding fact which emerges from all this is, as we noted in passing in the course of the argument, that human labour has ceased to be the measure of output in production.

Mr. Herbert Hoover, speaking just before he began his term as President to a conference of Associated Chambers of Commerce in America, put the basic fact very clearly. The productive equipment of the United States, he said, could now provide per head of population the same wealth of commodities as in the year before the war, and stand down two million men then necessary but now superfluous for its production. That he was not talking at random is clear from the confirmation given to his statement by the United States Bureau of Labour Statistics, which reports that since 1909 its records show an increase of 49 per cent in the average output per worker employed in all the factories in the States. In other words, for the volume of production requiring the human service of 100 men in 1909, all that is now needed is the service of 67 men.

This, however, is only the intensification over a few recent years of a process which had already wrought miracles of increased production. Long before 1909 the great main displacement of human labour from its position in the economics of production as a measure of output had already taken place; and the facts which Mr. Hoover gives us are only a two-hundredth new story added to what was already a skyscraper It was not until 1886 that the United States Government began to issue carefully collected statistics as to industry; and in the first annual report issued in that year by the Commissioner for Labour Statistics it was pointed out that American power-machine production was then employing four million workers, with an output that could not have been produced by fewer than 21 millions in pre-machine times. To put it in Mr. Hoover's way of presenting the facts, America by 1886 was able, in producing its then volume of wealth, to do without 17 million men who would once have been required for its production but had become unnecessary at that stage in the development of the power-machine. Add transport to actual production, and the official estimate was that the work done by the power-machine and on the railways in the United States in 1886 would have required the labour of three times the then total man population of America if the power put into it had been limited to human physical energy with man-handled tools.

The enormous change which the advent of the power-machine made in this respect at the very beginning is most dramatically revealed by the facts as to the textile industry in Lancashire. By the middle of last century, when the machine had been developed sufficiently to enable one worker to be allocated to 2,000 spindles, production by machine had so far escaped from the limitations of human energy that an output equal to the entire output of all Lancashire at the beginning of the process was producible by power-machines with only 25 workers required to supervise them. If our present textile output had to be produced within the limitations of human physical energy by handlooms and spinning-wheels, the entire population of these islands would hardly be able to provide the necessary labour.

The change wrought at the very outset by the substitution for human physical energy of these non-human energies in production was tremendous in extent and revolutionary in character. But while the impact of these energies upon our immemorial methods of compelling Nature to yield sustenance to mankind carried us straightway into a new world in which the factors and conditions of the struggle were fundamentally altered, it was only a beginning. The chick, though born gigantic, did not break out of its shell full-grown. Its gigantic immaturity was a fit beginning for the entry into human service of powers so incredibly beyond the imagination of a world limited in its conceptions of work to the poor performance of human muscles; and its growth has been continuous and proportionate. Enormous as was the immediate change, the earlier power-machines were crude and feeble manifestations of what was latent in this new thing that had come to assist mankind in subduing Nature to human requirements—mere museum pieces by comparison with our present-day equipment—and the new powers could only be used crudely and feebly. The intervening period has been one of incessant development; and by the standard now reached, the things which seemed so immense and amazing to the generation of first discoverers and users of the new powers seem to us almost comically ramshackle and ineffective. But the considerable gaps which still remain in the power-system, and the almost daily record of how they are constantly being filled in, make it pretty obvious that our own stage of achievement in the application of the new powers and their development towards automatism will in the same way provide the museums of the future with their examples of things outgrown.

Such facts as Mr. Hoover gives us reveal the unchecked rate at which that development still proceeds, and how the remnant demand for human physical energy which still survives in the processes of production is being steadily absorbed into the power-system. Side by side with the American figures can be placed the facts as to the development of manufacturing industries in Australia. In the 20-year period 1907–1927 the number of workers employed in Australian factories increased from 249,000 to 467,000: an increase of 87½ per cent. But the total yearly output rose from £87 millions to £347 millions; an increase of 300 per cent. These money figures of output, however, must of course be corrected for the change in prices between 1907 and 1927. As they stand, they show that while one worker was required for every £349 of output in 1907, only one was required for every £743 of output in 1927. Great as the shrinkage of labour in relation to output has been, it has obviously not been so great as that since 1907; the bulk of this apparent output-per-worker increase is accounted for by higher prices and not by volume of output. The necessary correction for prices shows the actual volume of output to have risen about 105 per cent, and the volume of production per employed worker to have risen therefore about 20 per cent. This is substantially less than the American figure, but all in the same stream of world tendency.

The pace at which the shrinkage of labour in relation to output goes on varies considerably between country and country, and is accelerated or retarded by political considerations, the attitude and the degree of influence of trade unions and of employers' associations, and many other factors; and also between industry and industry, largely according to the technical problems involved. But while it goes on more rapidly here and less rapidly there, it goes on everywhere and in all industries. Turning from these national facts to the facts of particular industries, we may note that Sir Eric Geddes, speaking as chairman of the Dunlop Company to the annual meeting (1930) of his shareholders, told them that "the output per worker employed in all our factories, at home and abroad, is now two and a half times what it was five years ago"; production requiring the services of five men then requiring only two men now, three becoming superfluous; and this within a brief period of five years, and from a starting-point which seemed five years ago to be about the possible limit of development.

The reduction of the labour costs to 20 per cent only of the complete cost of making a pair of boots at the Bata establishment in Czechoslovakia repeats the same tale of recent and still vigorously continuing development. In 1923, Bata was employing 1,800 workers with a daily output of 8,000 pairs of boots. For 1930 his figures are 17,000 workers and a daily output of 120,000 pairs. Within seven years output has increased at so much a greater pace than labour that while one worker was required in 1923 for every 4½ pairs of boots per day, one only is now required for every 7 pairs. In one period of three months only, following immediately on the experimental introduction of new methods into a single workshop, an increase of 800 pairs a day passing through that particular operation was obtained—2,000 pairs instead of the previously achieved 1,200 pairs—with a reduction in the number of workers from 210 to 180.

The elimination of labour by the comparatively recent introduction of the mechanical stoker, and by the use of self-feeding arrangements for oil fuel in place of coal, would make a chapter by itself in the record; to which it is here a sufficient index to quote the announcement made by the authorities of the Cunard Line that the change-over from coal to oil enabled them to reduce the number of stokers in their service from 951 to 263.

Even agriculture, the last of all industries to seem likely to be absorbed into the power-system, moves in the same direction. Milking by machinery has only quite recently become really effective. The earlier machines a few years ago were crude and unsatisfactory, after the manner of most machines in their first tentative stage; but the milking machines now available are more effective, and incidentally incomparably more cleanly, than hand milking. The results of a series of enquiries into the effect of the machines with a herd of 26 cows were given in the May 1930 issue of the *International Labour Review*, the League of Nations monthly publication on labour conditions throughout the world. The labour time for the whole operation, including fetching and tying-up the cows, carrying the milk to churns, and washing things up after milking, was 277 minutes by hand milking, three men being required; and 102 minutes by machine, only one man being employed. For the actual milking, without the accessory fetching and carrying, the labour time was 156 minutes by hand and 43 minutes by machine. In the land operations of actual cultivation, a 3-plough tractor covers a daily average that leaves the plodding ploughman far behind; and where but a few years ago files of men bending to the labour of scythe-swinging made their slow way across and across the harvest field, with a population of accessory workers gathering up armfuls of the cut swathes and binding them into sheaves, the new harvester and binder machine now clatters its rapid way through the task. Our little fields, plotted and fenced for hand labour, still obstruct the effective use of available machinery on a large scale; the cutting and threshing of forty acres of a wheat crop in one day, as is done on Canadian wheat farms with only two men required, is beyond our present achievement; but here as elsewhere the development goes on apace.

I need not multiply instances further. Over the whole range of production the amount of human labour embodied in each unit of product is constantly shrinking. Where the power-machine has been developed to automatism it has dwindled to an almost microscopic insignificance. In electric generation, for example, it would only be expressible as a minute fraction in relation to the unit of output. And according to the stage of advance of the power-machine towards automatism—an advance which, as we have seen, is going on rapidly in all industries—labour steadily diminishes in relation to output. The function of measuring output is transferred to the non-human energies and the mechanical equipment of industry for trapping and using them.

It is this shifting of the function of measuring output from labour to the non-human energies whose enslavement for human service defines the Industrial Revolution, it is this which, I submit, is the profound change to which we have failed to adjust our distributive system, and by that failure brought upon ourselves our present economic and commercial confusions. And it is to the elucidation of this that I now crave your attention for a little.

CHAPTER VII

Before discussing it in detail, it will be well, by way of placing the problem in its proper perspective, and for our guidance in that further discussion, to make a little digression at this point in order to get a clear grasp of certain fundamentals. The most defective economic arrangements from the point of view of general human welfare can be perches and nesting-places for special interests, and every economic discussion is complicated by the insistence with which such interests regard the conditions of their own survival as conditions necessary for keeping things going at all. One or two main direction-posts may be useful in keeping us to the track and avoiding these dead-ended byways.

The first essential thing upon which we must keep our minds centred at every stage in the enquiry is that the whole problem arises from the vast expansion of our resources consequent upon the escape of production from the limits of human labour. It is not a problem of insufficiency, but of a new and almost incredible abundance.

The Industrial Revolution has carried us into a new world in which the possible provision for all human needs has increased to such an extent that the old channels for distributing it into use and consumption have become incapable of fulfilling their function. They have not merely failed to convey the volume of possible production into the world's life, but have broken down under the strain, and turned the very abundance of our resources into confusion and trouble for us; precisely as an aqueduct which breaks down when suddenly called upon to carry a volume of water a thousand times beyond its capacity turns the countryside into a quagmire, floods people out of their homes, and spreads chaos and destruction all round by the very plenitude of the provision which, effectively conveyed to them, would be a blessing to the great populations athirst for it.

Lord D'Abernon has put the point very clearly. Speaking of the industrial prospects for 1931, he says:

> The economic crisis which to-day oppresses the business world is the stupidest and most gratuitous in history. All essential circumstances—except financial wisdom—favour an era of prosperity and well-being. Crops are more abundant than ever before; science has developed production beyond all precedent; inventiveness has discovered new processes in industry, increasing the power of man over nature, and enabling him to produce more at less cost. But the incapacity to adjust vehicle to burden, and means of payment to requirements, has brought about a crisis, so that many are starving in a world of plenty, while all are oppressed with a sense of depression and of incapacity to meet the situation. The explanation of this anomaly is that the machinery for handling and distributing the product of labour has proved quite inadequate.

If we are not clear to begin with as to this essential character of the world's trouble—that it is not our poverty but the marvellous expansion of our wealth to which we have to adjust our economics of distribution—our enquiry will be futile. In a world of scanty resources and meagre powers, of hard and narrow natural limits to our possible production, we should indeed have to consider economic problems as a matter of cutting our coat according to our cloth, and living within our scanty means. The problem we have to face to-day is the exact opposite; the problem of enabling the world to live up to its new abundant means.

The root fact of the whole matter is the fact of our escape from that world of scanty resources and meagre powers and hard and narrow natural limits to our possible production; the world in which all mankind had to fight for a bare living against what then seemed to be the cruel niggardliness of nature; the world of man's ignorance of the natural possibilities which lay hidden in profusion all around and about him. Hard drudgery could only extract a very little return from that tiny cache of the vast bountifulness of nature to which men had the key of knowledge in pre-scientific days. Their only working power was the feeble power of their own muscles, and their only tools the meagre appliances which they could operate by that working power; with the individual strength and skill of each man as the maximum unit of power which could be applied in the struggle with nature. The utmost co-operation could not, under such conditions, have made it other than a hard and a bare life.

Only now for the first time in human history can we speak of an opulent life released from drudgery for the whole community as a possibility for which the means are visible and at our immediate service and command. That possibility has come within sight and reach only as science has unlocked one after another the hitherto concealed treasure chambers of nature, giving us the entry of knowledge to new resources in power and materials, and in devices for using them to the uttermost for the service of human needs. Our trouble is not on that side at all. It is that our business devices for handling these resources still remain essentially the devices of a small-production economy, and have broken down under the weight of our new powers, to which they are hopelessly unrelated.

In considering what action our present distresses demand from us it is, therefore, vitally important that we distinguish very clearly between the limits which nature fixes for men and the obstructions which men set up for themselves in this matter of the possible standard of living. The special interests that profit by our existing confusions are constantly suggesting that there is a force of economic law behind the business devices and purely artificial methods of our distributive system; and since these are the very matters that require adjustment, we cannot be too alertly on our guard against such attempts to warn us off from dealing with them on such a plea that laws we cannot alter make them inevitable.

It is our productive capacity, and our productive capacity only, which fixes the limit beyond which our standard of life cannot go. If nature gave us few resources and scanty powers, our productive capacity would be inexorably limited to that narrow range; and we should have to go short and make the best of what little was within our reach. In such circumstances it would be futile to kick against a natural law by demanding a life more spacious than the available resources permitted. A common life of poverty would be natural in a poor world.

But poverty and insecurity in a world of abundant resources and of gigantic powers which have been effectively mastered and put in harness for human service is a monstrous stupidity. It is not a deprivation imposed upon us by any lack of natural opportunity, but a failure in human intelligence. Given the resources, their distribution is not a question of natural limits or inevitable laws from which we cannot escape, but of ordinary sensible human arrangements.

The practical importance of making this distinction very clearly will be obvious to anyone who takes note from day to day of what most politicians, economists, and commercial experts say about our present business confusions. What crops up constantly in all such talk is this suggestion that certain mysterious economic laws are responsible for what is happening. When the aqueduct breaks down in one of the periodic crises of overproduction into which its inequation with our producing capacity is constantly plunging us, our orthodox economists—that is, the economists whose business and interest it is to defend the existing system—assure us that the inevitable and inexorable laws of political economy make such a breakdown certain if we are foolish enough to produce beyond the carrying capacity of the aqueduct. That would be the plainest of plain common sense if what they meant was that a breakdown is inevitable if you attempt to use a conduit inadequate for the load you require it to carry. But that is not what they mean at all. What they insist upon is that the economic law is in the dimensions of the conduit itself, and that it is our producing activity which transgresses the law by pouring an excess into the conduit beyond those dimensions. The sacred and untouchable things, according to this, are the business and finance devices by which our economic system distributes purchasing power and rights of consumption; and to those devices our production must accommodate itself or come upon disaster. Their advice to us, therefore, pontifically announced at such times as a law of political science, is that we must economize and live within our means; our means, in that view of the matter, being the fractional part of our capacity for production which is allowed to pass into the world's life by the inadequacy of our distributive system.

Let us get our minds perfectly clear about this. Such a view of things is the view you get by standing on your head and seeing the world upside down. The plain fact is exactly the reverse. It is the conduit, the system of distribution, which is the thing alterable at human will; all its business and finance devices are human artifices subject, without any hindrance whatever other than lack of human intelligence, to any modification required for the better service of human needs. It is our productive capacity alone which sets any limit of natural law to our possible standards of living.

To invoke, as so many politicians and economists do

constantly invoke, "the inevitable and inexorable laws of political economy" for the working of a defective distributive system, is sheer nonsense. The world is under no obligation of economic law compelling it to accept the artificial scarcity and unnecessary deprivations of a faulty system of distribution. And all scarcity is artificial which is below our producing capacity. A distributive system is a faulty system which conveys our means to us by any less measure than that capacity.

It is the aqueduct which must be made capable of carrying the available supplies; and not the supplies which must be restricted to the carrying capacity of an insufficient aqueduct. The supplies are subject to natural law and natural resources, and have expanded enormously with our expanding knowledge and command of those resources. The construction of an aqueduct that will carry the load effectively instead of restricting it and recurrently breaking down under it, is subject to no limit other than the limit of ordinary human intelligence. To set ourselves to make men believe that they must remain poor in a world of abundant resources because the laws of economy inexorably forbid us to devise an effective carrier system, is to attempt the impossible. No sane man will or can believe it. The belief that the resources of the world can be got into the life of the world is axiomatic to human reason; and it is below the level of ordinary sanity to suggest the contrary.

In all this it is necessary also to guard our minds continually against confusing our productive capacity

E

with our actual production. The eminent German economist, Dr. Adolf Weber, professor of political science at Munich, in his defence of our present distributive arrangements, falls headlong into this confusion, and most of the minor prophets among the economists follow him. He argues quite seriously that "if all the goods produced were equally distributed, relatively little more would fall to the share of each person than a workman receives to-day." That may be true. I suspect that it is true, because it confirms the main charge against our distributive system. That main charge is not that it fails to pass on to the consumer—with constant friction, much waste, and periodic dislocation of the markets—what we actually produce; but that it prevents production, keeps it far below capacity, effectively prohibits it beyond the volume of the restricted distributive conduit possibilities.

As I pointed out to begin with, our producing system takes its orders from the consuming side, and is governed in its output by the distribution of purchasing power and effective consuming demand. It does not produce in response to any estimate of human needs. It produces to meet the available purchasing demand in its markets, and the distribution of that effective purchasing power of demand is ridiculously below the level of human needs. Consequently our production is also ridiculously below human needs, in accord with the sparse distribution of purchasing power. To think of actual production under such conditions as being the same thing as capacity for production is a merely grotesque confusion of mind. Without any further increase in our knowledge of power and of technical processes, or of our available materials, we could multiply production ten times over if the needs of the world were permitted to express themselves in effective demand.

Under the restrictions of our distributive system we dare not use our powers of production for fear of glutting the market and bringing about a general crash of financial interests. The condition of glut is not in any way related to the human need for our product. It is a glut only in relation to the restricted purchasing demand in the market. With the present low standards of living of vast populations, far below the requirements of a full life, with widespread poverty and deprivation all the world over, it would be idle to talk of any glut in relation to the possible and desirable human use of products. It becomes glut and over-production only in its bearing upon the possible marketing profits the financer of production can get by selling his goods; and the possibility of such profitable marketing vanishes when the supply of goods outweighs the purchasing power in the market.

Production is not governed by the economics of use, but by the economics of profit; and is therefore kept down to the limit of profitable selling fixed by the distribution of purchasing power. To such extent as that distribution is below the level of human needs, to the like extent is production also kept below capacity; and our available resources in a world of plenty are thus restricted to the meagreness of our distributive system instead of expanding to the fullness of our producing capacity. If for only six months, and without any addition to our existing equipment, all the power plants of the world were to work to their full capacity, every market, from the point of view of profitable selling, would collapse under the weight of unmarketable commodities which the distributed purchasing power would be incompetent to take up; and every market would still be inadequately supplied by the test of human needs.

Incidentally you will find in this the simple secret of those cycles of good and bad trade of which our economists so often speak as though we were subject to some inexorable law of periodicity in the conditions under which nature yields livelihood to man. The periodicity and the occasions for it are exclusively in the business and finance arrangements of our distributive system. What actually happens is neither mysterious nor inexorable, but, as Lord D'Abernon bluntly tells us, merely stupid and gratuitous.

Our production is governed, not by the economics of use, but by the economics of profit. That is to say, it is production for the finance purposes of our system of ownership and distribution; never set going by the stimulus of serving known human needs, but only by the expectation of collecting financial values in marketing. When the beginnings of a trade revival are observed this expectation grows. The finance and business interests controlling production begin to command output beyond immediate ascertained orders in the hope of finding or making a market; every competing business unit in the finance of production being anxious to get in on an expanding market while there is elbow-room. The movement gathers impetus; new finance enterprises and fresh capitalizations are floated, until it grows to the stage when new companies almost daily join the glad throng that goes marching along to the expectation of profits, and the trade boom is at its height. At which stage the wise financer unobtrusively gets out, leaving the late comers, whose throng is greatest just then, to hold the baby.

Why does production not stay at that height, seeing that the needs of human life are so great that our producing activity even at the boom point still falls short of them? For the simple reason that human needs have nothing to do with the matter. The purpose of it all is the collection of financial values from the markets; and financial values can only be collected when they have been distributed as purchasing power to the mass of the world's people. But all capitalization comes into the economic system in the form of a debt from the producing activities of the world to the financing interests; a standing charge upon the ultimate product, a charge to be collected in prices from the consumer. Such capitalization involves the forms of ownership and finance which are our distributive system; and what is distributed as purchasing power to the mass of the world's people through the restricted channels of this system of ownership and finance is never sufficient to absorb the flow of product at the prices required if the finance system is to recover its charges from the market.

We will look into that rather more closely later; but

the cycle through which things must revolve with such a distribution of purchasing power unrelated to the financial values to be recovered from the market is obvious. What begins as a gently increased flow of commodities into the channels of distribution becomes accelerated and swollen to a flood. The point of maximum expansion of the restricted channels is soon reached; production becomes overproduction in relation to distributed purchasing power; and the distributive system breaks down under the load. The unmarketable surplus of commodities for which no equivalent purchasing power has been provided turns the trading world into a quagmire once more; production is checked back again to narrow limits; and the cycle revolves from good trade to bad trade and depression until the quagmire is sufficiently dried up to prepare the conditions for beginning the same process all over again.

The economists describe it to us as the process of "leaving it to the operation of economic laws to effect the proper balance between production and market consumption"; the assumption, as you will notice, being that the finance and business devices of our economic system are the fixed and irrefragable things and producing capacity the errant thing which must be thrown back into conformity with them. What it means, quite simply, is putting up with a great deal of human suffering, insecurity, and the periodic dislocation of life because we choose stupidly to hamper ourselves with a distributive system hopelessly incommensurate with our powers of production; so hopelessly that every time our new immense powers are given any inducement to try to serve us up to their capacity, the thing goes to pieces.

Get production going with anything like a swing towards full capacity, and what comes of it is not the natural result—an enrichment of the world's life with supplies—but an economic crisis in which all the forces of bankruptcy and disaster are brought to bear upon production to compel it to curb its mistaken idea that its business is to produce with amplitude. It gets the same moral addressed to it, and feels the weight of the same big stick, as the tormented toad in the old story: "I'll larn you for being production!" And we are all sharply reminded that, having acquired our new mastery of the powers and resources of the world, we shall be flying in the face of political economy if we are foolish enough to use them fully.

All of which procedure, while it may be very sound and orthodox political economy, seems uncommonly like lunacy; or at any rate somewhat lacking in that broader sanity of purpose in human life to which we shall have to equate our economy if we are to survive as a civilization at all.

* * * * *

We should now be able to resume our detailed enquiry with a somewhat clearer sense of general direction. It should also be clear to us at this stage that if our enquiry is to lead us anywhere at all, it must be concerned with very fundamental things. What is wrong is evidently at the roots of things, and not merely in detail. That should be obvious from the fact that both in practice and in precept our existing economics are at variance with certain quite simple and elementary conceptions as to life and its purposes which for most people are axiomatic in the very nature of things; conceptions which most of us feel we could not abandon without abandoning our sense of reason. Such axioms seem to me to be these:—

That the ultimate sane purpose of production is to supply the goods and services required for satisfying human needs as fully as our productive powers permit;

That the function of a distributive system is to ensure, with the least possible difficulty and obstruction, the passing of produced wealth into the use and consumption for which it is intended;

That while our producing capacity is governed by the natural laws and facts of the world we live in, by our knowledge of its resources and our power to apply that knowledge, distributive efficiency is simply a matter of human arrangements and is not prescribed or limited for us by anything other than the intelligence with which we make such arrangements and administer them;

That since there is no natural law or compulsion whatever which disables us from effectively distributing into its proper use and consumption what we are capable of producing, if in fact and experience we do find ourselves so disabled the reasons for that are necessarily in our own defective and inadequate methods, which can be discerned, defined, and corrected.

And the incontrovertible facts of the problem in relation to these simple axioms would seem to be:—

That in actual fact and experience we are now so disabled;

That the distribution of purchasing power is so inadequate as to leave a vast mass of human needs unsatisfied to the point of acute distress and poverty for great numbers of people and of anxious insecurity for nearly everybody;

That since production takes its orders, not from the needs of human life but from the extent to which people with needs can express their needs in effective purchasing demand upon production, our distributive system, by the inadequacy to which it limits that demand, checks and discourages production instead of assisting and stimulating it;

That our actual production under these conditions is enormously below our producing capacity, which has expanded and is expanding per head of population to an almost incredible extent; and though this expanded producing capacity has never been permitted to test itself against the full demands which human needs might make upon it, it is unquestionably a capacity for satisfying those needs upon a scale vastly greater than the inadequacy of distributed purchasing power now permits it to attempt.

These are the indisputable facts; and if they are admitted, as indeed they must be, the form which our questioning must take is clear and obvious. For what such facts show is that our distributive arrangements are not serving the purposes of distribution; that they are obstructing and thwarting the intentions of a distributive system instead of performing them. They are not only unrelated to human needs, but also to human power of supply; and since the first essential of an effective distributive system—its very definition, surely—is that it should be the servant of human needs up to the fullness of human power of supply, this want of relationship to either is a complete failure to function; and reveals our distributive system as a system for preventing distribution instead of promoting it. As it thus works out in practice it ceases, in short, to be a distributive system at all and becomes the exact reverse; a hold-up system by which the life of the world is condemned to poverty and want in the midst of abounding resources.

In such circumstances we cannot take the soundness of anything in our distributory arrangements for granted. We have to scrutinize them exhaustively. How is purchasing power, in fact, distributed? Since it is unrelated either to human needs or to human power of supply, to what is it related? By what processes and through what channels does it flow into the world's life and become available as effective command over goods and services for the person into whose possession it comes? And how are its recipients selected? What are the recognized titles to its possession and apportionment? Somewhere in the mesh of such questions, if the net of scrutiny is drawn closely enough, we should find some clue to the secret of our failure to enable the world to consume what the life of the world is in dire need of and is equipped with ample knowledge and power to produce in response to that need; a failure which, seen in its simple relationship of means to ends, would almost seem to be capable of no other explanation than that we are bewitched, and under one of those spells that prevent a man from doing so simple a thing as putting one foot before the other, or lifting the food from his plate to his mouth.

CHAPTER VIII

The only way in which we can get our questions answered is by examining the facts; and the facts which have the clearest immediate bearing upon the problems are the facts as to unemployment. For the unemployment problem is where we come upon our distributive arrangements, directly and without complications, in the act of cutting off supplies wholesale from masses of people. Here we get to the deeper depth which proverbially exists within every depth. What unemployment means is that for millions of people throughout the world it is no longer a question of the poverty of employed life, the sparsity of distributed purchasing power in the ordinary course of rendering service within an economic system, but of being outcast altogether from the category of those to whom the normal distribution of purchasing power, whether sparse or otherwise, takes place at all.

The immediate instinct of all of us, taking as we do familiar and long-established things for granted, is to retort at once: "Of course they do not share in the normal distribution of purchasing power; they have ceased working." But if, in view of the admittedly calamitous way in which our distributive system does in fact fail to function, we are to follow our rule of taking nothing whatever for granted in connexion with it, we must, I think, begin our scrutiny of unemployment by looking at the assumption implicit in that retort .axiomatic as it may seem to be; an assumption which we cannot allow to pass unquestioned, since with it the clue to what we are seeking may possibly slip through also and escape us.

Why do we almost instinctively assume that ceasing work should necessarily mean ceasing to participate in the normal distribution of purchasing power? It is true that our natural human sense of things is not so obliterated by our economic assumptions that we ever really think of being unemployed as ceasing to have the right to live; but this natural human feeling that we cannot allow people to starve is the feeling of a duty of charity devolving upon ourselves rather than the admission of a claim based on any economic right.

The reason for this is obvious. The mind of a world accustomed through all its recorded ages to the fact that the supply of all the material satisfactions for its needs has been dependent upon and measured by the exercise of human labour makes such an assumption almost automatically. But is it an assumption we can reasonably continue to make in a world in which, as we have seen, the fundamental change which has taken place is the substitution of other powers for human physical powers as the energy of production? Is it an assumption that can remain unmodified when, for the first time in human history, human labour has ceased to be the measure of output? Clearly there is matter for very close scrutiny here at the very outset.

In such new conditions it is obvious that our old intuitions, confirmed and rooted in us by age-long experience, may mislead us altogether. Must we not—all our inherited traditions and axioms notwithstanding

—begin by recognizing the plain fact that these new forces mean dispensing with human labour; and that the economics of power-production must differ profoundly from the economics of human energy and handicraft production by their allowance for and adjustment to the fact that power-production in its very nature is a vast reduction of human labour in relation to output? The distribution of claims to consumption cannot remain unaffected by so profound a change in the conditions of production. Human life released from labour in this way, with a greatly increased supply of everything needed for human life forthcoming as a result of such release, clearly cannot continue to be regarded as necessarily condemned to deprivations.

With the supersession of human labour by other powers as the energy of production, and the consequent measurement of output by the scale on which these non-human energies are applied—human labour becoming, in proportion to their application, less and less relevant to volume of output—we have completely changed the basic factor in the problem of distribution. It is a basic factor no longer related to the human labour exercised in the production of wealth; and all the edifice of distribution founded upon conceptions of consuming rights as being necessarily associated with producing energy and measure of output in the exercise of human labour, has become detached from the realities of life. We produce now by methods which steadily diminish and diminish the immemorial compulsion upon mankind to labour for the satisfaction of human needs, coupling with that release from drudgery the gift of vastly larger satisfactions than the drudge-age of human existence could have dreamt of; so gigantic is the energy of our new slaves, dwarfing our old human energy of production to insignificance. A revaluation of our basic accepted ethics in the economics of distribution is imperative.

As for the prevalent illusion that power-appliances, while they reduce labour in relation to each unit of output, by that very process cheapen production and stimulate consumption so greatly that more and more employment will always result from their use, it is an illusion which collapses under any serious and penetrative enquiry. That a world-wide equipment for and use of power-machine production leads—and must necessarily lead under the restrictions of our present distribution system—to the relegation to unemployment of a constantly increasing proportion of the world's population, is a truth which is not in the least degree controverted by noting that up till quite recently power-producing nations did in fact expand their employed populations on a big scale. The facts show conclusively that we have now passed beyond that initial stage in the development of power-production. It was the stage at which the possession of power-producing equipment was confined to but a few countries; and while it lasted it concealed the cessation of human employment which is implicit in the nature of the new powers; concealed it by giving to those few countries a whole world of outside markets into which their gigantic product could overflow.

At first England had practically a monopoly and became the workshop of the world; and it was because English production was production for the world's consumption that English power-appliances provided employment for a rapidly expanding industrial population. In the nature of things such a monopoly could not endure, if only by reason of the fact that knowledge and the applied use of knowledge cannot be kept confined to its place of origin. But in this matter there has been from the beginning an economic compulsion upon the nations using power-production to set up their market countries with equipment for similar production on their own account. To the nature of that compulsion, and how it has contributed to our present troubles, we shall return. It is sufficient at this point to note that, whatever may have been the impelling causes, the countries of the world which were markets for the overflow of the vast output of the few power-producing countries have in fact themselves become power-producers; that the new production has become established everywhere; and that its world-wide establishment has brought us to the stage in the development of the Industrial Revolution at which its full effects in the supersession of human labour have to be tabled without any chance of the old concealment by overflow.[1]

[1] The old objection of the manual worker to machinery, which has so often been laughed at as baseless by economists, is at last beginning to prove that it has some foundation. American economists have given a new name to a certain kind of unemployment, and call it "technological," by which they mean that it is due to rationalization and the efficiency of machinery. In other

One country with the world as an overflow for its power-products naturally had an almost unlimited scope for the expansion of its population and their employment. And even as another and another and another of the market countries for which the original universal provider catered became themselves power-producers, outside markets in so wide a world still remained vast enough to provide, though with a growing stringency of competition, some sort of overflow for a time for the earlier comers. But only the simplest prevision was necessary at that stage to discern what must come of it. With a dwindling remainder of outside markets and a growing army of power-producing communities competing for them, it became more and more difficult in any such community for the inherent "less and less human labour in relation to output" consequences of the power system to be cancelled by the enlarged employment resulting from a world-wide overflow for products; and we have now reached the stage at which—with competition intensified to the savagery of war, and practically every remaining undeveloped region of the world absorbed into the political system of some one or other of the big producers as an outlet for trade—a proportion of the people of every industrialized nation are unwanted, and their unemployment has become the outstanding problem which civilization has to face everywhere.

words, our economic arrangements are so ill-adjusted that in all the leading countries of the world widespread distress is apparent, simply because the production of wealth has become so easy. The position is so absurd that if we cannot rectify it our civilization deserves to perish. (Mr. Hartley Withers.)

And still unremittingly with every week that passes, the process by which any given output of wealth requires less and less human labour for its production continues.

This spread of power-production throughout the world has swept on at a constantly accelerating pace; and it is worth a somewhat lengthy parenthesis in the main argument to note some of its details. Its most significant development has been amongst those vast Asiatic communities—India, China, and Japan—which between them account for about half the entire population of the world. The swiftness with which these great markets and overflow areas for the power-products of the industrialized white nations are being transformed into competitors keen both upon supplying their own home needs and scrambling for a share in outside markets with the rest of us, has its most striking example in Japan. Mr. Inouye, Japanese Minister of Finance, in a memorable speech in 1929, summing up what had been accomplished, closed with the declaration that "so far as Japan's national economy is concerned, we are transformed from an agricultural to a commercial and manufacturing country." Within fifty years, this which within living memory was a remote and detached country of peasants with ways of life strange to all the outside world, has become one of the foremost of the world's communities in all manner of power-production: iron and steel and machinery, shipbuilding, textiles and paper, chemicals and dyes, electrical development, and every variety of the activities to which the new forces of the

Industrial Revolution have given birth. It has run rapidly through the phases of financial reorganization associated with such a development; and its trade shows the usual current of a developing industrialization—increased food and raw materials and decreased finished goods for its imports, with the process reversed for its exports. The capitalization of its manufacturing industries—which reveals the scale of its equipment for power-production—was 833 million yen in 1914 and 4,642 millions in 1927. Its annual manufacturing output rose in the same period from 1,371 millions to 6,947 millions. The Central Bank of Japan began in 1926 to issue a monthly index of employment; and these indices are an illuminating revelation of the "more and more wealth with less and less labour" tendency inherent in power-production. Taking the year of the first returns, 1926, as the standard year at 100 index figure, the general average of employment in all the chief industries of Japan fell to 94·8 for 1927 and 90·3 for 1928. The only group of industries showing an increase of employment was the heavy industries group, an increase explained by the fact that Japan was during that period producing her own machinery on a great scale and ceasing to be a customer for it; Japanese imports of machinery falling from 128 million yen in 1924 to 78 millions in 1927. In the spinning industry, the fact that the technique of power-production has been more effective all the world over in eliminating the need for human labour than in the average industries is reflected in the fall of the Japanese index of employment from the 100 of

1926 to 82·2 in 1928, a fall substantially greater than the general manufacturing average. "Yet," says Mr. Seishi Idei in his *The Unemployed Problem in Japan*, "there has been no proportionate decrease either in the number of spindles or in production, and this points to the rapid progress made in rationalization."

All the leading characteristics of the general power-production development of the world are here plainly visible; the expansion of equipment, the falling ratio of employment to output, and the constriction of the market for outside manufactured products as its own equipment expands. And with it all—since Japan came into the development at the late period when the effect of power-production in making human labour superfluous could no longer be hidden by overflow into outside markets on a scale big enough to put men into work more quickly than power-production puts them out—with it all a chronic problem of unemployment.

There is no need to multiply instances. The fact that there is no industrialized country without its problem of unemployment is conclusive as to the stage of unconcealment of this necessary consequence of power-production which we have reached. And on precisely similar lines every part of the world is speeding up with its equipment for power-production. Mr. Hsein Fong, in his *Extent and Effect of Industrialization in China*, tells us that notwithstanding the political confusions of the country, "we are supplying an increasing proportion of our own needs; our imports are changing from manufactures to raw materials; we need less manufactured goods"; a view quite confirmed by the facts in detail, such as, for example, the increase in the number of spindles operating in Chinese textile establishments from one and a half millions in 1919 to well over four millions in 1928. The same sweeping tendency is shown in the increase of the capitalization of manufacturing industries in Australia from 80 millions in 1908 to 303 millions in 1925; and the astonishing increase of similar capitalization in Canada, which started rather earlier to emerge from its agricultural colonization phase of life, from 78 million dollars in 1870 to 3,500 millions in 1924.

Textile equipments, with their vast outputs in relation to labour employed, and the universality of the need for which they cater, are a good index to the spread of power-production throughout the world. Since the war and up to 1929, amongst the later European entrants into the industrial arena, Finland showed an increase of 21 per cent in looms and Poland an increase of 36 per cent. Japan's increase has been 298 per cent for the same period, and China's 409 per cent. In spindle power Japan's increase is 183 per cent, China's 256, and Brazil's 129. India was already well advanced with textile power-production equipment before the war, and the percentage of increase is therefore not so great there; but it was a 43 per cent increase on spindles and a 77 per cent increase on looms.

Percentages of increase, when reckoned on the development from small beginnings, would, of course, be quite misleading if they were taken as indices of comparison between actual equipments. But the significance of such percentages of increase as these is quite apart from any comparisons of that sort. Their significance is in their revelation of the pace at which the previously unequipped countries are becoming independent of outside production; the rate at which the world is becoming covered with power plants, and consequently the rate at which the overflow areas of the world are disappearing. The economic situation in which the factors are a few power-producing countries in a world of virgin markets is one thing; a power-producing world is quite another. For into what outside markets can its products overflow on the vast scale necessary to put its armies of superseded workers into employment again? Without adding anything to its present equipment—by using its present equipment to full capacity—it could provide for all its needs on a lavish scale and still not encroach unduly on the leisure of its people, released as they are in such large measure by the processes of power-production from the requirement of human labour. But, as we have seen, it cannot produce on any such lavish scale without commercial breakdown; the spending power which it distributes by its present methods is not adequate to make a market for the goods it produces. And it must, while that inadequacy of distribution continues, have markets outside its own producing economy—within which the defective distribution occurs—into which the otherwise unmarketable surplus can overflow. The notion that, in these circumstances, power-producing industrialism on a world scale can look for any trade revival to set its unemployed populations to work again is mere fantastic illusion.

The point can be finally illustrated by what has recently happened in the Lancashire weaving industry. It is Sir James Jeans who, if I remember rightly, in one of those absorbingly interesting books of his on *Our Mysterious Universe*, by way of illustrating the emptiness of space, tells us that the remoteness of each star from its neighbours in the depths of space is comparable with the remoteness of each wasp from the others if three of them wandering about Europe were the entire wasp population of the continent. I do not suggest that human workers in our huge weaving sheds in the textile industry to-day are quite so sparsely scattered about as that, but the analogy quite grotesquely insists upon obtruding itself on my mind; and certainly any one who visits a modern weaving shed for the first time expecting to find it a thronged hive of busy people will have something of the feeling of solitude about it as he surveys the array of automatic looms in vista with the occasional human attendants distributed scantily among them. But in the incessant movement of power-production nearer and nearer to automatism a further development has taken place. New power looms, of which a regiment of twenty can be supervised by two human workers, have been devised. Even by their limited use somewhat below that capacity, it is claimed for them, as a result of full experiment, that their introduction will bring about a reduction of at least 25 per cent in the labour costs of production and a proportionate gain in efficiency.

The weavers have been making a desperate attempt to resist their introduction, and for the moment their development has been held up. And Mr. J. L. Garvin, reasoning with the workers on the hopelessness of such resistance, says: "Everybody knows that its first consequence must be a redundancy of labour. But our real problem is to carry the surplus of labour through the difficult period which must elapse before the expansion of markets enables it to be re-absorbed into a regenerated industry."

It is true enough that labour opposition to its own elimination by the introduction of such machines is in the long run hopeless. It is the pathetically futile attempt of men who live by being employed to resist processes which diminish the need for their employment, processes which are implicit in the nature and inevitable in the development of the new non-human powers and appliances to which the functions of energy and skill in production have been transferred. But is Mr. Garvin's expectation of markets sufficiently expanded by cheapness to re-absorb the displaced labour of the world into employment any less hopeless in its refusal to face facts and to grasp their significance? In this particular case the plain fact is that if Lancashire were to expand its markets up to the high level of the biggest boom ever known in the textile industry, the development of power-production represented by these looms would still leave half the weavers of Lancashire unemployed and superfluous. And with a world-wide equipment of the old customer nations for power-production on their own account and on a similar scale, the notion that any one nation will ever again expand and establish its markets stably on the old "workshop of the world" footing is sheer credulous illusion. Lancashire itself knows better than to nurse any such irrational expectation. Mr. Naesmith, the secretary of the Weavers' Association, in a statement issued at the New Year on the prospects of 1931, says: "The desire of former customers to satisfy their needs with their own products proceeds apace; and we must face the fact that the industry has definitely contracted, and that never again will it find employment for the same number of people."

It is necessary, however, that we should at this point closely examine this view of how prosperity is to be restored and industry regenerated. It is the view upon which there is a general insistence; the current discussion of our troubles is little more than a reiterated assertion that this is the only way. And an exposure of its illusion and fallacies will not only reveal its ineptitude in relation to the facts, but will take us effectively into the next necessary stage of our own enquiry.

CHAPTER IX

For any return to prosperity our first need, in this view of the matter, is the utmost possible cheapening of production by every available device of rationalization and improved technique of power-production. It is admitted that the first effect of this must be to make more labour redundant; because these devices and powers, in the usage which our present economic system makes of them, can only secure cheaper production by reducing the number of men whom it is necessary to hire and maintain for any given output. Each man so hired accounts, in association with the improved machine or the rationalized organization, for passing a greater quantity of material and a larger volume of complete products through the processes of manufacture. Only so far as that is achieved is the machine or the organization of any advantage to the financers of manufacture in cheapening production, or its introduction of any use to the economics of their business.

But while the first and admitted effect is thus to render more labour redundant, if a demand for more output can be created the redundant labour will begin to be re-absorbed in proportion to the increased output. Such a demand for more output can only come by cheapening production sufficiently to enable the financers of manufacture to compete successfully with their rivals in the world's markets, and by that successful competition to increase their sales and orders.

And with the need for greater output in response to such expanding orders, the ultimate result will, it is claimed, be a revived and regenerated industry, not only able, but by the demands of its restored prosperity compelled, to hire the redundant labour once more.

It is further pointed out that for any return to prosperity on these lines, it is essential that this same process of reducing labour costs should also be applied to the public services, and what are called the sheltered industries of the country; that is to say, the activities in which labour has to be hired for purposes not directly concerned with production for the world's competitive markets. The financers of the competing manufacturing industries have to buy much service and equipment from these sheltered industries and public services; and in purchasing the service they need from, for example, the building trade, or transport service from the home roads or railways, or indeed any home activity not subject to outside competition, they have to pay prices based upon the costs of such home services, which thus become costs of manufacture entering into the prices to be recovered from the ultimate purchaser for whose custom they are competing in the outside markets. In this way the cost of, say, sewerage or police protection or any other public service paid for by a levy of rates or taxes becomes part of the cost of production in the manufacturing industries, and a factor in the ability of the financers of production to compete in the world's markets. The policy of reducing labour costs must, therefore, be an all-round national policy, and not something special to the competing industries themselves. Without this corresponding general national policy, the efforts made for cheap production in the competing industries would be in large measure nullified; and it is to such an all-round policy of reducing labour costs that any nation must therefore look for revived prosperity.

Let it be admitted at the outset that there is nothing else open to us but to try it out on these lines if our present economic system is to be accepted as the basis of our activities. We must settle down grimly to this competition in which the nation to emerge triumphant will be the nation whose working population will produce most and live on least. *Per famem vinces.* There is no other way within the limits of our present economics of ownership and distribution. There is, indeed, as we shall see, no suggestion in it for varying the procedure of our present economic system, but only for applying that procedure with such intensity as to enable it to work to its full and unrestrained capacity; and if its utter hopelessness can be demonstrated, as I think it can be, what is demonstrated is the hopelessness of the system itself, and not merely of a particular way of operating it to which other alternatives would, in the event of continued failure to meet the world's difficulties, be left for trial. There are no other alternatives.

You will have noted that throughout this brief statement of the case we have to examine I have spoken always of "the financers of manufacture" and not of "manufacturers." That is not a mere wilful change of terminology, but a matter of real substance with a vitally important bearing on the whole discussion. It is an attempt to distinguish rather more clearly than has, I think, hitherto been done in economic discussion, between the producing and the distributive function in our industrial economy; and it is necessary to explain it a little more fully.

The essential distinction between the producing and the distributive function is that the one has to do with the intrinsic qualities and uses of things, while the other has to do with financial values. The manufacturer as manufacturer has to do with such problems as the qualities of materials, their applicability to the various needs of human life, the effectiveness of power in relation to the handling of commodities whose ultimate purpose is use; in a word, the technique of making things. It is in that aspect of things that the Industrial Revolution has effected its enormous change in the work and life of the world.

But the moment you begin to discuss problems dealing with costs, prices, sales, market conditions, or any matter involving financial values, you pass out from the producing system proper into the economics of distribution and ownership. The manufacturer of boots, for example, must, in his capacity as manufacturer, be concerned with such questions as the qualities of leather, the ways in which it reacts to tool or machine processes; in short, the whole technique by which a boot becomes suited to a human foot. But when he concerns himself with costs or prices or sales, it is as the financer of manufacture, and in pursuit of another purpose altogether than the effective making of boots. He ceases to be concerned with boots as boots; and is only concerned with them as containers and carriers of financial values. He has financed their production by the capitalization of his business, and when they are completed they are not essentially boots to him, but receptacles in which all the costs he has had to meet during the process of manufacture are locked up. They represent the financial values sunk in the business up to the point of their completed production.

All such costs during production are related, not to any essential problem of production itself, but to selling and marketing possibilities in relation to prices; and all questions of selling and marketing are questions, not of supplying boots as boots to people who need them, but of recovering in prices the financial values locked up in them. Production as production is a very varied and intensely interesting thing, having to do with the intrinsic character of commodities; but all business and commerce is essentially the same thing, having to do with financial values, and only with particular commodities as the counters and markers of financial values.

The case for intensified cheapness as the only way of restoring prosperity is wholly confined to this financial aspect of things. It relates exclusively to questions of costs and prices. It has nothing to do with the technique of production as a technique of production, but only with its relative cheapness and the calculations as to financial values which have to be made in regard to it; nor has it anything to do with labour as human life, but only as a cost of production, an eater-up of the financial values expended on its hire, which have to be included in the cost of production and recovered in prices from the purchaser of the ultimate product.

All this is the working mechanism of our system of distribution and ownership; and this usage of our powers of production so as to conform to the financial values requirements of the distributive system is the only usage permitted to us within the existing economics of distribution and ownership. And since the whole purpose of our enquiry is to discover how and why our distributive system has so egregiously failed to relate itself to the changed technique of production as to leave the mass of the world's people—as indisputably it has left them—poor in face of the superabundant possibilities of plenty of which the new power-production is capable, it is obviously of the first importance that we should keep the two things—production and the financing of production—separate and distinct in our minds.

It is all the more necessary and at the same time perhaps easier to do so because the two functions have in fact very largely ceased to be identified with the same person. As I have pointed out, the manufacturer of boots must, in his capacity as manufacturer, be greatly concerned with the producing technique of his business, as technique apart from financial values. And so no doubt he did concern himself while he was an individual. Over pretty well the whole range of manufacturing industry he has now become a company of shareholders, hiring the services of a technical and managing staff for the work of production proper, and concerning themselves only with the financial aspect of things; transferring their holdings from one form of production to another on considerations of financial values only; getting out of railways to buy cottons, out of cottons to buy iron, out of iron to buy rubbers, and out of rubbers—if they got out in time to get out with anything left for other buying—to whatever else may have presented greater possibilities of collecting financial values from the world's markets. "Financer of manufacture" has in these circumstances become the only accurate term; not only for purposes of precise description, but also for purposes of precise distinction between production as an end related to human needs and production as an activity subservient and subsidiary to the real end pursued by the financer of manufacture; an end quite clearly revealed by the fact that, if his business is to achieve his real purpose in it, what you have to ask him is not, "Are you making boots?" but "Are you making money?"

There is, as I have already pointed out, no suggestion in the case presented to us as a recipe for prosperity for varying in any way the procedure of the present economic system. All this handling of the commodities necessary for the world's life, not by methods primarily designed to interpret and meet the world's needs, but according to the financial requirements of competitive commerce for cheapness based on the reduction of hired-labour costs, *is* the procedure of our distributive system. It is in the course of such operations that all rights to consumption are distributed, and the character of the distribution—inclusion in it or exclusion from it, and in what relative proportions—determined. What we have to examine is the claim now made for this distributive procedure that—notwithstanding the admitted distresses and confusions by which the world's life has been persistently afflicted under it; its utter failure as a distributive system to pass on into the world's life the possible plenty of which our producing powers and resources are capable, failure of which the standing evidence is the continued poverty of the mass of people in a world equipped with such powers; and the recurring check upon the use of our powers by which it throws production back into bankruptcy and commercial disaster whenever we venture to produce plentifully—what we have to examine is the claim that, notwithstanding all this, it contains the secret of prosperity for any nation in whose industrial life these same methods, which have so far resulted in these afflictions, are developed with still further intensity up to the point of such cheapness in production as will give it a competitive advantage over its world rivals.

The first thing to be noted about it is that there is no recognition in it of any common world problem in our present troubles. It asserts the possibility of a local and national escape from evils which all the facts show to be related to common causes in a world system of economics. In a world in which every industrial nation is suffering from similar evils of poverty, insecurity, and unemployment such a common experience sets up the strongest presumption that the causes are to be sought and found in the economic system which is common to all of them. The evils are the same everywhere, varying in degree but in their lowest degree serious everywhere, and in character identical; and they are in evidence, not only at times of special trade depression, but at the highest levels to which our economic system ever permits trade to recover before shattering it again in the cycle by which trade recovery always leads to so-called over-production. What is suggested to us is that the financers of manufacture in a single country, using the methods of the economic system within which these results are everywhere displayed, can by an effort of competition against their rivals in other countries achieve a separate prosperity of their own; and that their prosperity, achieved by such a process of reduced labour costs, will create a prosperity for the common life of their country; regardless of the reactions of such success—assuming it to be achievable—on the life of the world and its recoil on the life of the successful country itself.

The new governing factor in the problem, be it remembered, is that equipment for power-production and facilities for cheapness are no longer the exclusive possession of one or a few countries, but have become world-wide. And our problems of unemployment have arisen and grown to their present intensity as this world-wide extension of power-production has developed.

Let us note very carefully, therefore, the conditions

that now have to be faced by any one of the older power-producing countries which seeks to recover for itself something of its old "workshop of the world" command of outside markets so as to re-absorb its redundant labour into employment.

It is imperative, under the usage of power-production prescribed by the finance of our distributive system, that there must be outside markets. There are two reasons for this; the first a perfectly natural reason in the nature of power-production; the second a much more sinister and world-disturbing reason in the defective distribution of consuming rights under our present economic system.

The first of these reasons is very plain common sense. Without power-production or facilities for power transport, the old handicraft and peasant communities had to produce within their own locality pretty well everything on which they lived, and each thing only in the small volume capable of being consumed locally and within their small human-energy capacity for production. But power-production, far and away beyond the limitations of human energy, can and does turn out any commodity in vast quantities which cannot be consumed locally, even though the needs of everybody in the locality for that particular commodity were gorged to the full; and this excess of particular commodities can, by exchange for similarly produced excess of other distant communities, enrich the menu of life everywhere with a variety of new satisfactions drawn from all the climates of the world. Thus in Finland, with its native timber, the reels on which the housewives of the world get their sewing cotton are turned out in dozens of millions, of no use whatever to the people of Finland without an outside market in which they can exchange their excess of reels for oranges from Palestine, rubber from Malaya, tea from Ceylon, or any other commodities they desire and cannot produce for themselves. That is the natural and beneficial use and need for outside markets; a need related to the consuming capacity of the people producing an excess in this way, and having for its function at the end of the process the return to them of their excess of special products transformed into more varied human satisfactions than their own local products would give them.

But the second reason why outside markets are imperative under our present economic system is, as I have said, much more sinister. It is that consuming rights, within the community in which the surplus is produced, are so distributed as to leave the vast mass of human life with insufficient purchasing power to make a home market either for the surplus itself *or for its equivalent* in any commodities for which it might be exchanged. We shall see in very precise detail how that comes about when we come to examine the workings of our economic system with a view to dissecting out the causes of its failure. Meanwhile it is of the utmost importance that this distinction between the two factors which compel the commerce of every power-producing nation to seek outside markets should be noted with the greatest possible clearness. Many people seem to imagine that the first—the natural and beneficial—reason for seeking outside markets is the only one; forgetting that it only operates as a beneficial process when the rights of consumption within the exporting nation are so distributed as to enable the equivalent of the exported surplus to be received and used. The real urgency of the thrust for outside markets arises from this second and graver cause, the inability of the home market of every developed industrial country to absorb the equivalent of its own output. All that, however, we shall have to explore a little later; at the moment it is sufficient to note that the finance of the system requires an expansion of its markets beyond its own home area; and that the whole competitive scramble and urgency for such markets—an urgency which does not stop short of the menace of war itself for the sake of markets—is evidence of the vital need for them in our existing economy.

The world-wide extension of power-production has completely changed both the range of and the conditions of access to such outside markets. Instead of a few power-producing nations competing with one another for the right of supplying vast customer communities unequipped for supplying themselves with industrial products, we now have a world in which the previous customer communities have become so equipped; and are not only protecting their own home markets against the incursion of such products from outside, but under the compulsion for outside markets which characterizes the whole system are also seeking overflow areas for an export trade of their own. They, like the older producing nations before them, are compelled by the finance of our economic system to recover in prices larger financial values than they have distributed as effective purchasing power within their own home markets. What was an open market for industrial products thus becomes a market carefully guarded against outside supplies of competing products, and at the same time a new competitor for the dwindling remainder open markets of the world.

In a brief reference to this process in an earlier section, I pointed out that this rapid development of power-production throughout the world is not simply due to the fact that in the nature of things knowledge and the applied use of knowledge cannot be confined to its place of origin, but that there has from the beginning been an economic compulsion upon the trading nations to set up their market countries with equipment for similar production on their own account, and to turn them from customers into competitors. The nature of this compulsion by which an industrial producer is first of all under the necessity of finding outside markets and then, as soon as it gets them, under the necessity of closing them again by setting them up with a competitive equipment against itself, should now be obvious.

For the same fatal flaw in our distributive system which compels it to seek outside markets because it does not distribute a sufficiently effective purchasing power in its own home area to permit its product to be taken up, also forbids it, as we have seen, to take its payment from these outside markets in goods to be brought back for sale in its own home markets. Obviously, if the products which have to be exported in the first instance cannot be absorbed by the home market because of an ineffective distribution of purchasing power, neither can goods imported in return for them. Very largely the trading nation has to take its payment by investing it as capital in the outside country and financing its development. That is why the older industrial nations such as Britain become creditor nations with vast investments abroad. The extraordinary complications which have finally resulted from this economic compulsion to promote the development of customer nations belong to a further stage in the enquiry: I am only concerned here to note the fact of such compulsion, and its sequel in the fact that no market country can, under this necessity of our economic system, remain a market country, but must, by the action of the supplying nation itself, begin at once to be capitalized for industrial development.

President Hoover has put the point quite clearly. "We have," he says, "an equipment and a skill that yield us a surplus of commodities for export, for which we cannot usefully take compensation by way of imported commodities. There is only one remedy, and that is by the systematic permanent investment of our surplus production in reproductive work abroad." And this explains that quaint and curious phrase—in which at first glance all common sense would seem to be inverted—"a favourable balance of trade" as defining the commercial position of a country which sends out more in exports than it receives in imports.

In the seven years from 1922 to 1928 Great Britain in this way exported £668 millions more than its imports; and the United States of America in the single year 1928–29 exported £200 millions more than its imports. It does not mean, as the simple-minded might imagine, that the financers of manufacture in these two countries sent their products out without getting payment for them, but that they took their payment in the form of investment in the capitalization and development of the outside countries. Whatever might be inferred to the contrary from the export and import figures, the first law of commerce—that all financial values deposited as costs in any product during the course of its production must be recovered in prices from the consumer—has been duly complied with.

In these ways and with great rapidity the development of power-producing industrialism has now extended over by far the greater part of the populations of the world; and continues with such momentum and at such a pace as to ensure a general equipment of all the world with the labour-eliminating power and devices of the Industrial Revolution. And it is under such conditions that Great Britain is invited to believe that a further cheapening of British labour costs of production is all that is required for recapturing world markets for British trade and such a regeneration of British industry as will re-absorb the present redundant British labour and give us a general national prosperity.

It is a suggestion which has no sense of world realities in it; and is, indeed, obviously made more by way of attempting, in special relation to the crisis in the weaving industry, to reconcile British labour to the admitted immediate certainty of becoming further redundant, than by way of serious thinking on a serious problem. For in the first place the expansion of the market would need to be on an enormous scale to serve any such ends. The non-human power now available in production is so gigantic that in this case of the Lancashire weaving industry and the new looms a world trade beyond all "workshop of the world" records in any industry would still not make it necessary to hire more than a fraction of the redundant human labour. To make any real impression upon unemployment, trade expansion would have to go out and away beyond all that. And the conditions for any such expansion of outside markets no longer exist.

Two conditions essential for such expansion are at once obvious: that the nation achieving it must possess a secret, not only of cheapness in production, but of greater cheapness than its rivals can command, and be able to put its goods upon the markets with smaller financial values embodied in them to be recovered in prices than other producers are under the economic necessity of recovering: and that the markets of the world must remain open to the products of that cheapness.

Would they? Do they, even as things now are? Assuming it to be possible for one competing national unit to secure and retain an advantage of cheapness over the others, is it conceivable that the others—now practically all the rest of the world—having committed themselves to a career of industrial production, will leave their home markets open to that sort of competition? The existing tariff walls of the world are a sufficient answer to any such credulous hallucination. Without such protection, industrial production could neither establish nor maintain itself in any country against a power of cheaper production in another country to whose goods it continued to give the right of access at prices below its own costs of production. To admit such competition would be to expose its own industries to extinction and to revert to a peasant career of primitive industry.

The methods of and equipment for the cheapest available production are open to all the world. The markets in which an outside producer could hope to operate with an advantage of cheapness against the home producer are first the markets in which home industrial production is in its earlier stages and the small volume of output means a greater cost per unit of product—the markets which all the world over are now the most sedulously guarded by tariffs for fostering the growing industries—and second those older markets in which social services and a comparatively high standard of living for labour have been established, and higher costs of production thereby incurred. That such countries—if the existing economic system continues—will come to a choice between tariffs and the abandonment of their social services and higher standards of living for labour, seems to be evident from the drift of their politics just now. The United States of America, having decided for tariffs, have discovered that to be no guarantee against the disastrous consequences of an outworn and defective economic system; and the Free Traders who in Great Britain are preaching the other alternative—a stringent economy which in effect means the cutting down of social services and standards of living—will find that to be no guarantee either. But no doubt in the political field, in which catchwords and the surface appearance of things count for so much more than fundamental underlying realities, this superficial controversy will continue to attract the attention of a public with whom the study of underlying realities is not popular.

The "workshop of the world" idea belonged to the period when but a few power-production units existed in a world of vast virgin markets. As a practical possibility, the capture of markets on any such scale by any single national unit is as extinct as the dodo in a world equipped to all its horizons with facilities for similar cheap production. The competitive advantage of getting above the head of the crowd by mounting a stool of rationalization and the cheapening of labour costs is all very well when yours is the only stool or one of only a few stools; but it disappears when every other unit in the crowd has an identical stool at his disposal.

It is worth while noting, in passing, that if such a permanent advantage in cheapness were possible for any one competing unit as a basis for its own prosperity by the capture of the world's markets, the likelihood of the British unit being that one is very small. The reasons for this have been set out in a very lucid and convincing way by the National Federation of

Engineering and Allied Employers. On behalf of the British engineering industry, the Federation has recently issued a remarkable statement of its difficulties. "British Engineering," it tells us, "is in a very grave position. The sales of its products are declining, and with increasing rapidity. Unemployment is high, and is still mounting. The outlook is as dark as the present." It supports that gloomy opening statement with a wealth of comprehensive statistical facts which leave no standing room for any doubt whatever as to the sombre truth of the picture; and on these ascertained facts it goes on to discuss the question of labour costs and their possible reduction; the core of its argument being that the finance of British industry is permanently, and to all appearance unavoidably, handicapped in any effort to compete for the markets of the world by certain natural conditions to which life is subject in this country.

The point is one of quite outstanding importance in its bearing upon the general claim we are now examining that prosperity for this country depends upon the effective cutting of our labour costs of production to such a point as will enable the finance of our industries to put products on the world's markets at prices which can successfully outdo our world rivals. If it be true that British failure to do so is due to natural and unavoidable conditions—and the case put forward by the engineering employers leads to no other possible conclusion—it is a conclusion of momentous importance indeed to all British industry in its relation to any competing effort to restore national prosperity on these lines. It is, therefore, necessary to set it out with all possible clearness.

The argument begins by admitting the fact that the general equipment of the world for power-production has put the whole problem of effective competition on a new footing. "Many other countries," we are reminded, "now produce goods which they either did not produce at all before the war or did not produce in the same quantity or quality." Not only have they "started their own industries instead of buying from us," but they have become exporters against us in the world's markets. And the vital point is that some of them are able to pay "cash-wages much lower than in this country."

"Cash-wages" is the keyword to the whole matter. For, as the engineers go on to point out, lower cash-wages do not necessarily mean a lower mode of living for labour. "It is clear that in a climate where little or no heating is required, where rope-shoes can be used instead of much more expensive leather boots and shoes, and less and lighter clothing is worn, less money needs to be spent in such ways." The coolie, in the realities of comfort, gets a standard of living equal to that of British labour; but he gets it in large measure gratis from the climate, while British labour has to spend cash on warmth and weatherproof shoes, on more substantial clothing and housing and other things necessary to secure the standard of comfort of which the coolie gets this large margin without requiring to spend money on it. But, as the engineers with unanswerable truth go on to remind us, "it is the difference in wages *paid in cash* which adds to the cost of our production. For the cash paid in wages and in social services is part of the cost of the goods, and has to be repaid by those to whom we sell."

The coolie needs smaller cash-wages because many of his human requirements are not cash-requirements as they are to British labour. He gets an equal mode of living without needing equal cash-wages to buy it with. But his smaller cash-wages determine the cost of production with which the finance of British industry has to compete. British industrial finance, paying the necessarily higher cash-rates of hire for British labour, has in that way to lock-up in its products larger financial values for subsequent recovery in prices from the markets than its competitors need to do. It is difficult to see how any competing level of British cheapness can be achieved in such circumstances. The reduction of the cash-rates of hire for British labour to the coolie level would seem to be the only way; and that appears to be a natural impossibility unless we can breed a new working class in this country, with its flesh and blood impervious to cold and to weather conditions. If our thoughts turn in that direction, we might as well go the whole way and explore the physiological possibility of breeding a working class capable of living without eating, and so reduce the need for cash-wages still more effectively, and give to our finance of manufacture such low costs of production as no rivals could compete against—until they also have learnt that secret of cheap production.

The machine responding to the impact of non-human

powers does, it is true, give us something of that sort in such degree as it approaches automatism; and in an entirely real sense the new weaving looms, for example, are a working-class impervious to cold and weather conditions, and clear of the nutriment expenses associated with a flesh and blood working-class. But unfortunately for the achievement of the full ideals of our economic system in the matter of reducing the costs of production, the human attendant upon our new steel and power workers is still in some degree—happily for financial values a diminishing degree—a necessary cost of production. And whether the British climate is regarded as a cost of production to British industrial finance, or the warmer climates of the world as a subsidy to the industrial finance of our rivals, the practical result is the same: a standing natural handicap to any British effort of effective competition. It would seem, therefore, that if it were possible for some one nation to achieve control of the world's markets by outstanding cheapness of production, not only Britain but every competitor similarly handicapped by having to add costs of climate to its prices, would have to submit to an economic hegemony of the world by the financers of production in those regions where the human requirements of labour need the least cash purchasing power for their satisfaction.

No such world market expansion is, I submit, any longer possible. From the outset our economic system has been incapable of serving the needs of human life on the scale made possible by the new giant powers now available for human service. From the outset, the prevailing standards of human life under its operations have been a dwarfed mockery of disproportion to the life a system of distribution adjusted to our new powers of production could easily give us. And we have now reached the stage at which an economic system thus hopelessly incompetent from the first of supporting the weight and volume of such production as our new powers have made possible, has come very nearly to the end of the incessant out-buttressing process by which alone it has been able to survive so far under the weight even of the poor use it has permitted us to make of those powers.

The root fact is that it does not distribute in effective purchasing power the financial values it is compelled to collect from its markets. Its whole purpose is to collect in prices a surplus of profits beyond the financial values with which it equips its home markets with purchasing power by distributing payments for human services during the course of production. These payments for services are the labour costs of production which have to be reduced to the lowest possible point in relation to output. But they are also the basic consuming rights by the exercise of which prices are recovered from the markets. Hence the home market always has a top-heaviness of output from the producing system which those consuming rights cannot carry; and so has to be buttressed by outside markets to serve the finance needs of the system.

As Mr. Hoover puts it, commodities cannot usefully be received from the outside markets in payment for much of the surplus sent out to them. How should they, seeing that the surplus so sent out is sent out in large measure because the home market has no consuming rights to cover its equivalent? Since, therefore, a considerable portion of these financial values recovered in the outside market cannot thus "usefully" be brought back in commodities, it remains in the outside market, which by its investment becomes developed and equipped for similar production; and so the buttress becomes itself a further protuberance of top-heaviness, to be in turn buttressed by further outside markets subject in their turn also to the same development. And as the world is limited, there is an end to that process; the end which is now becoming plainly visible; when the system, always resonant with the crash of local bankruptcies, grows into a world-wide single system within which consuming rights do not exist in proportion to output, and becomes itself bankrupt by the spatial impossibility of any further effective out-buttressing. And what now remains for us is to explore with precision this non-distribution of consuming rights in relation to output which is the source and origin of the whole economic trouble of the world.

CHAPTER X

We must, I think, approach this core of our enquiry by examining the primary purposes and outlooks of our distributive system—the ends to which it works—before passing on to its detail. The details are only the working mechanism by which a purpose becomes effective. We shall not understand the details when we come to them, they will seem meaningless and crazy, unless we see them in relation to the purpose they purport to serve, and see that purpose itself in relation to the needs and possibilities of the world's life.

The moment we begin such an examination we are conscious of an immense conflict in our civilization; of antagonistic forces straining against one another in human affairs. For quite obviously the need of the world in a system of distribution is that it shall distribute, shall pass the possible resources into full use and consumption. Equally obvious are the possibilities; our new technique of production stands recognizably as the means by which such resources have expanded and can expand into more and more abundance available for human life. So far as our powers and resources are concerned, there is no problem at all, but the plainest of plain certainties that provision can be made for all the human needs of the world. Our difficulties, therefore, are not with the provision of wealth; but with getting it into consumption, and with the barriers which our methods of getting it into consumption set up against its production beyond a fraction of what it could be.

On the one hand we have a new technique of production which gives us a vastly greater output of all the requirements of life with less and less need for human labour in proportion to its output; and on the other hand, an economy of ownership and distribution which cancels out the purpose of this release of human life from drudgery by making the consuming rights of the mass of mankind still dependent upon the continuous requirement for the exercise of their labour; shutting them out automatically from any claim to consuming rights at all if it does not need to hire and employ them; and, when it has to hire them, measuring their right of consumption by wage-payments related only to the cash-cost of living. Their only claim to consumption is this wage-claim for maintenance while the machine requires their attendance upon it. And in the working of the machine under our present economics of ownership and distribution, the incessant endeavour is to make their attendance required less and less in relation to output; to increase output while diminishing this labour charge upon it, and so to produce more and more cheaply. In a word, to bring each unit of product to completion with less and less labour claim to consumption distributed against it.

The advance of civilization in new knowledge and power applied to production stands essentially for service to and expansion of human life. But the handling and control of this new knowledge and power by our present economic system reverses all that. The human right to consumption, distributed as payment for hired labour, becomes a cost of production, and affects financial values detrimentally by increasing costs; and so the very thing which reason tells us is the central purpose of civilization—the endowment of human life with the widest possible satisfactions—becomes, as a cost of production, the thing which has to be cut down to the smallest possible margin of maintenance for the vast majority of mankind. Instead of human life expanding to the measure of output, it has to be kept rigidly down, when transformed into "costs" in this way, to the lowest possible proportion to output; and the whole sane human intention in production is thereby reversed. For one has to ask, in such circumstances, what is production for except to provide abundance for mankind? Quite clearly that is not the purpose in production of our present economic system, under which the mass of mankind have no right in it at all when the technique of production gives us the abundance by the measure of other powers than their labour; their maintenance being regarded as a burden of costs against it to be reduced as greatly as possible.

Here, therefore, is a clash of purposes in our civilization, which cannot continue without ultimate breakdown. No social order could stand the strain of such an internal conflict for long without disruption. Implicit in the nature of our productive powers is the philosophy of life which asserts that in a sane world abundant resources mean the possibility of abundant life. But the philosophy and outlook on life of our economic system is a philosophy which, both implicitly and in the actual tragedy of practice, denies to human beings as such any right to live other than the financial and economic right created by the system itself. In practice this means for the mass of mankind a right solely dependent upon their attendance being required on productive machinery which constantly develops towards a greater automatism and less need for their attendance. Thirty millions of unemployed people in the industrial countries of the world stand to-day outcast from the right to consumption under the operation of this system; dependent on public or private charity and mendicancy; and in every such country the financers of industry are clamouring for the abolition or restriction of the social services through which that public provision is forthcoming, on the ground that such a distribution of maintenance to those whom the economic system no longer needs to hire puts, by rates and taxes, a crippling burden of unnecessary costs of production upon industrial finance. Implicit in the whole working of the system is this denial of the human right to live.

This view of the relation between human life and the world's resources is inherently absurd. Scrapping human beings because the financial machine of our economic system cannot provide for them in a world of ample resources is to make the machine the central purpose of the world's life. But human beings and the satisfaction of their needs are assuredly the central purpose of the world. Man does not exist to serve the needs of an economic system. An economic system exists to serve the needs of man; and if it does not serve them, it is the system and not the human life for which it fails to provide that has to be scrapped. That millions of men and women cease to have any right or claim to live because science has given us the power of producing increased satisfactions for human life by other means than the employment of human labour, is a proposition about which we need not argue. When new powers and methods of production have been developed which serve the needs of men abundantly and efficiently with a diminishing requirement for their own labour in the process, all that has to be said about the suggestion that they thereupon lose their right to live is that it is a suggestion outside the range of ordinary sanity.[1] The sane conclusion is that the ethics and economics of a system of ownership and distribution which produce such results have themselves become obsolete, and are no longer related to the facts of life and the methods by which the world's needs can be supplied.

Obviously this is not a matter of mere adjustments within the existing economy, a simple lopping and pruning of its dead wood. The facts as to the supersession of men by power-production and the obsolescence of human labour as the measure of the world's wealth available for use and consumption are an axe at the roots. The change imperatively demanded by such facts can be nothing less than an entirely new ethic in distribution related to and in harmony with

[1] Read the City articles in the great newspapers, and you will ask yourselves if you are not living in a lunatic asylum. The answer is that you are. (G. Bernard Shaw.)

the entirely new method by which human satisfactions are produced. The Industrial Revolution, on the showing of such facts, is as yet incomplete and one-sided. It has given us the means of an enormous expansion of the enrichment of life, with no corresponding development in making that enrichment accessible to life. We can produce, but we are prohibited from consuming. If we do produce according to our new powers we throw the world's affairs into confusion by overproduction and the world's people into resourcelessness by unemployment. We can turn on ample supplies in such measure as to make poverty a ridiculous anachronism, but we have provided for ourselves no channels of carriage and irrigation by which to pass the supplies on into the life of the world. The clear and imperative demand for such a situation is a revolution on the distributive side corresponding to the accomplished revolution on the productive side. Without such a corresponding new order in distribution, the new order in production remains thwarted and ineffective for its purpose of the enrichment of life.

No conclusion carrying with it such implications of fundamental change is ever very readily accepted. Even when the facts on which the conclusion is based are overwhelming, many people will shut their minds against the clearest possible proof rather than face a fundamental issue. But here the facts are not only conclusive to reason; they have become the realities of discomfort and insecurity in life for such a growing army of hitherto comfortable and secure people as to compel an attention which reason by itself might not command.

The whole economic system labours along with such constant conflict and friction, such a shocking want of adjustment to the needs of life, such incapacity to translate natural plenty into human satisfactions, as to set up at any rate a strong presumption of inherent defects rather than a simple want of lubrication. The fact that we have such a problem at all as poverty in an age of power-producible plenty—that we have it, not in exceptional conditions and limited areas subject to special difficulties, but persistently and everywhere as the normal established condition of life for the mass of mankind—goes to strengthen the presumption of something at fault in the essentials of our economy, and not merely in its occasional aberrations and localized conditions of maladjustment.

But habit and familiarity are very powerful. We do not begin our experiences of life with fully matured powers of observation and judgment. We are born into it and grow into it. Our observation is at first entirely without judgment, a simple absorption of experience. The facts around us soak into our consciousness and establish themselves there as the necessary conditions of the world in which we find ourselves; and by the time our powers of judgment begin to mature we have got into the habit of taking the general scheme of things for granted as something to which critical judgment is not applicable. Detailed faults may be noted and remedied; but the thing as a whole escapes our critical scrutiny by this force of acquiescent habit, and we take it for granted as the natural order of things. Even when its pressure upon our lives becomes so intolerable as the pressure of economic trouble now is, forcing upon us the larger question whether the thing as a whole, the fundamental ethic of it, may not itself be the fault we have to remedy, we have to overcome an immense inertia of the mind against such fundamental questioning before we dare own, even to ourselves, the set of our thought in such a direction.

We have, I submit, come to one of those hours in human history when the facts of experience are implacable in leaving us no other alternative; an hour when the future of civilization depends upon our release from that inertia of the mind, upon our readiness to uncover and decide a fundamental issue.

At any time such inertia is dangerous; in critical times it may be fatal. Just as the geological record reveals to us the story of once great living species gone to utter extinction by reason of their inability to adjust themselves to a changed environment, the inertia and relative fixity of their physical system against the demand of new surroundings for fundamentally changed habits of life if the creatures were to survive; so also is human history littered with the records of once flourishing social structures gone to pieces by the same fatal inadaptability, the inertia against adjusting the order of their living to profoundly altered conditions. It is this inertia of habit hardened into an inertia of mind which petrifies old ways of living into fixed obstacles, preventing men from even thinking that fundamental questioning of established habits is permissible to them.

Quite incontrovertibly and beyond the need of further proof, the conditions in which we have to live our economic life have been profoundly changed. Power-production has made a clean breach of continuity in the economy of human living; as clean and decisive a breach of continuity as a geological convulsion makes when it lifts a land from swampy conditions to a more arid level and conditions of soil presenting a new problem of the means of life to all the creatures inhabiting the affected regions. It has substituted other powers for the power of human labour as the energy of production; and that substitution has entirely and fundamentally changed the character of man's struggle with Nature for sustenance. In the basic conditions of human access to and command over the resources upon which we live, the immemorial order of human life has been replaced by a new order; of which the defining characteristic is that human labour has ceased to be the measure of human supplies, and for it has been substituted the new gigantic and inexhaustible measure of non-human energy.

Quite incontrovertibly and beyond the need for further proof, our economics of ownership and distribution do not allow us either to use these powers to full capacity or to assimilate into human life the product of such cramped usage of them as it does allow. Under its operations, a degree of production far short either of the capacity of the new powers or the human need for satisfactions becomes what is ludicrously called overproduction, by which our whole economic life is repelled from further production and periodically thrown into confusions and bankruptcies.

Quite incontrovertibly and beyond the need of further proof, this so-called overproduction is not overproduction in relation to the world's needs. It is the permission given to the world's people to consume which is restricted; not the capacity for production which outruns the human need for consumption. It is our distributive system in the act of displaying its inability to cope with the new conditions of production. And in the interplay of this economic failure, chronic problems of poverty and unemployment associated with plenty have become world-wide.

The facts, the incontestable facts, establish beyond a doubt that what is wrong with our economics of ownership and distribution is not merely a want of adjustment in detail which can be remedied, but a basic and essential incompetence to implement the needs of civilization under power-producing conditions. And we must continue our scrutiny with a complete assurance that it will be futile unless we continue it with minds tuned, as I have said, to the uncovering and decision of fundamental issues.

CHAPTER XI

In stating the thesis of this book at its beginning, I put the proposition that our distributive system remains, in its essential character, the old system of the pre-science age of the world; that its economics would be seen on examination to be the obsolete economics of that now vanished period in human history when human labour power was the measure of the possible output of wealth for human sustenance and enjoyment; and that we should find the explanation of our troubles in the fact that our economics of ownership and distribution are unadjusted and inadjustable to the new period in human history to which power-production has brought us, the period in which non-human power has become the measure of our possible provision for the satisfactions of mankind. Our producing capacity with these new powers has become, in ratio to the human labour needed to make it effective, a ton for every poundweight it was before the Industrial Revolution; and we are still trying to deal with its distribution by the pound-packet measurements of the age of human drudgery.

Something of the purport of this should now be clear; something of the profound questioning of existing human relations to which such a proposition takes us. For the relations of men and classes in a social order are defined and governed by the economics of distribution; and when a conclusion is reached that an old economic system needs to be superseded by a new system based on new principles, the full statement of that conclusion must be in terms of the supersession of an old by a new social order of human relationships. And if we are still hesitant about believing that man, if he applies himself to the task, is as much the master of his own affairs in the shaping of a social order as in the building of a new house, so hesitant as to be fearful of uncovering such a fundamental issue, we may at least, before abandoning ourselves to that inertia, examine the facts clearly enough to know to what it is we surrender our power of decision and action and the possibilities of life.

The plain fact to begin with—the fact which is the subject of enquiry—is the failure of our present economic system to pass the abundance now available with power-production into the general life of the world for use and consumption. It is a system under which consuming rights are distributed to the vast mass of the people, not according to wealth available for consumption or the ratio of production to population, but by maintenance allowances made to labour services required in production.

But labour services required in production have ceased to be the measure of output; and such a distribution of consuming rights has therefore ceased to be a measure by which output expanded so gigantically beyond it can become the standard of the general life of the world; and must become less and less adequate for that purpose—which is the essential purpose of production—in the degree in which the ratio of production to population and the volume of products available for consumption continue to expand beyond this maintenance allowance scale of distribution; as in fact and in the nature of power-production they do continue to expand.

This applies not only to the human labour which has been superseded by other powers as the actual physical energy of production, but to all human services contributory to production. All such human services in a system of power-production—technical planning and management as well as the physical energy of labour—are devoted to preparing and maintaining the set of conditions into which the non-human powers can be introduced and within which they can do their giant work most effectively. Such human services throughout the whole process are the rubbing of Aladdin's lamp so as to call up the non-human powers and set them going at their work. This is the fundamental change which our discovery and command over these new powers has made in the character of the human effort required in production—that the measure of output is the measure of these new energies of production and not of the human services. It is the defining fact of the Industrial Revolution.

But though human service has ceased to be the measure of output, it still remains the sole creator of output, and the only means by which the larger energies which are now the measure of our production are harnessed and kept going at their work. Production remains our production, although its output has escaped from the energy-limits of our own natural powers. We produce by a new measure of power which is outside ourselves and not the capacity for labour in us, but it is we who summon and control that power, we who produce. From start to finish, through every detail of every anterior process before production comes to its final stage of the completed commodity ready for use and consumption—in the collection of raw materials and their preliminary treatment, in all transport, in the provision and equipment of buildings, in the making of machinery and in the generation of power—in all the ramification of production back to the stage at which every raw material for any of these things lay virgin in the resources of Nature, there is no point whatever at which anything enters or can enter other than human engagement in services which are finally materialized in the finished commodity. Human effort applied to natural resources—nothing else enters, and nothing else in the nature of things can enter into the making of any commodity. And although these natural resources, by the extension of human knowledge, now include for us not only inert materials but fertilities and powers which have superseded our own self-contained energies as the measure of the output, none the less it remains true that human effort using and controlling natural resources is the sole source of all the produced wealth of the world.

Up to this point you will notice that we have been considering realities only; the actual things; human beings, natural resources, actual products. Now let us restate the truth of that last paragraph in slightly different terms. Instead of saying that there is no point in all that ramification of production at which anything enters or can enter other than human engagement in services, human effort applied to natural resources, let us put it that there is no point at which any cost of production enters or can enter other than the cost of maintaining human services. The only possible real cost of production is the consumption of wealth which goes on amongst the people engaged in the service of production; the food and clothing and shelter they eat up or wear out, the material of every sort they consume or use up; in a word, the depletion of existing wealth by use and consumption necessary to keep life going while new wealth for use and consumption is being created.

That may seem to you at first sight to be merely saying the same thing over again. But it is much more than that. For when we begin to speak of "costs of production" we leave the region of actual things and become concerned with the finance of an economic system. The difference is so great that although at first sight most of us, accustomed to regard the finance of an economic system as a fact in the nature of things, would read the one statement as being only a repetition of the other, if amongst my readers there were a stranger from another planet, unacquainted with our economic system, he would perfectly understand the first statement, made in terms of real things, but would entirely misunderstand the second statement, made in terms of "costs."

And since it is upon an understanding on this point that an understanding of the whole working of our economic system depends, we shall do well to put ourselves in his place for a little, to see what his difficulties are, and how we could explain the thing to him; for in such an explanation we shall probably find the best way of explaining it to ourselves.

His difficulty would be that, not having any knowledge of our economic system, he would only be able to interpret "costs of production" by trying to relate them in some way to the natural facts of human life. The natural purpose of all production is the sustenance of human life. If it is not continually sustained by the use and consumption of existing wealth, it perishes; and life at any moment is, therefore, the consumption of wealth which up to that moment has been made ready for use concurrently with the preparation of further wealth for the continuance of life; the two things being incessant and inseparable in the texture of human existence as the essential condition of human survival. Constant using and constant replacement make the unity of enduring human life; the growth of life if the replacement is greater than the consumption, the decay if less.

What sort of meaning could our enquirer, with these natural facts in mind, attach to our talk of "costs of production"? "What is a 'cost'?" he would ask himself. The natural cost of a thing—and he would be confined to natural data in trying to discover what we mean—is what has to be given up in order to get it. What is it that has to be given up in order to get freshly produced wealth? What does the life of the world lose in exchange for fresh wealth? He would probably puzzle over that for a long time. It is doubtful, indeed, whether with only natural facts to go upon he would ever hit on the answer given by our economics; for it would hardly be likely to occur to anyone uninformed as to the finance implications of our use of the word "costs" in this connexion that any rational beings would think of what they consume as being lost to them. What they consume would present itself to his intelligence as the final and assured gain, the realized gain, which all production is intended to secure for us in the sustenance of life.

In the effort to defend and explain the appalling consequences of our economic system in human life, a great edifice of nonsense has been built up—in what purports to be the science of economics, but is really the apologetics of the system for the human misery it causes—on this point of the use and consumption of wealth while other wealth for further use and consumption is being produced; and one can only guard one's mind against it by getting down to the bedrock of realities. For the reality of things is that human life is continuous; and the consumption of previously produced wealth while new wealth is being produced is only the natural fulfilment of the purpose of the previous production. It is the continuous natural process by which life goes on; human life as a connected whole, yesterday, to-day, and to-morrow; and the consumption of wealth while other wealth is being produced is only the flow of life in the natural current of sustained existence. Life cannot consume what is not yet completed for consumption, nor complete that further provision without consumption of what has preceded it;

and the continuous life of the race is in this unbroken flow of sustenance and preparation for further sustenance going on together.

The description of this continuous process of consumption as a "cost of production" is, as we shall see when we penetrate to its full meaning, the clue to the sinister thing in our present economic system by which the world's life is kept in continual impoverishment in the midst of abundance. For the moment it is sufficient to note that in the actual facts of life the "labour costs" of our economic system are nothing other than the human life of the world in this natural sequence of continuous living; and that what is described as the "cost of production" is not a cost at all in the natural facts of human existence, but only the fulfilment of the purpose of production—the purpose for which the continuous work and life of the race makes provision; that purpose being consumption and the sustenance of life. It is only in relation to the claims of our system of ownership that the consumption of wealth by the mass of mankind during their production of further wealth—that is to say, the process of life itself—has to be reckoned as a cost of production. All such reckoning takes us from the realities of life to the finance of our present economics of ownership and distribution; the artifices of a social system based on these forms of ownership and distribution, and not the natural facts of life.

That, however, a little outruns the argument at this stage. Let us return to our enquirer, whom we left in the effort of puzzling out what our "costs of production" can possibly mean in relation to the natural facts of human life; and little likely to hit upon such a queer conception of "costs" as is involved in the idea that the consumption which gives us life is a cost of what we produce instead of the end to which we produce it; something we have to give up in order to get fresh production instead of the gain of continued life for continued activity. But suppose he did get an inkling of it. Constant use and constant replacement is the associated process of life; and it is just possible that, as the only interpretation by which we could be imagined to mean anything at all, he might relate our use of the idea of "costs" to the fact of replacement, and come to the conclusion that what we really mean is that we have some measure of relative values by which our needs of consumption are measured against output in order to ensure the necessary replacement; that we figure to ourselves this replacement as a debt we incur by consumption, as in fact it is; and that "costs of production" must mean some way we have of reckoning our consuming needs so as to equate our effort of replacement to them; our consuming needs, in the demand they make for a constant stream of wealth to be used up, being the only conceivable thing entering into costs by this debt-of-replacement way of regarding costs. He would certainly regard it as a curiously inverted conception of what "costs" are, but it would be the only imaginable way in which he could relate any conception of costs at all to the natural facts of life.

Such a conclusion shows how unintelligible all this costs and finance aspect of our affairs must be to anyone who tries to grasp its meaning with only the natural view of production as human activity for the satisfaction of human needs to guide him. For the only possible interpretation such an enquirer could give to it is, as you see, hopelessly wrong. So far from "costs of production" being a standard of measurement by which we equate our production to our consuming needs on a debt-of-replacement basis, the finance of our economic system is wholly directed to and dependent upon keeping costs of production down to the smallest possible proportion to output.

From the natural view of production as human activity for the satisfaction of human needs, any such disparity between output and consuming rights—for costs of production are nothing but consuming rights distributed against output—is, of course, an impossibility; a flat denial of the whole purpose of production. The only possible costs of production are in the consumption which accompanies production; in other words, in the maintenance of the working life of the world. And what conceivable purpose production can have other than the maintenance of the human life of the world, nobody taking the natural view of production could possibly imagine; for implicit in that view is the natural assumption that the working life of the world is the whole of human life, constantly consuming and sharing in the activities of replacement.

And that maintenance, be it noted, includes every sort of consumption which accompanies production. The general working life of mankind requires the consumption of corn by sowing it in the ground for a future crop as well as by eating bread; and in a power-producing world a great deal of consumption analogous to that is necessary—making machines and consuming them in use for further production—in the common flow of the world's activities. But, as we have seen, however far back and through whatever ramifications of preparation this production and consumption of wealth in the intermediate stages of production may extend, nothing enters into it or can enter into it at any point whatever other than the working life of mankind, human effort applied to natural resources. All such consumption enters into and is fully accounted for by the sustenance of the working life of mankind; and it is this consumption which our present economic system describes as the "cost of production."

When, therefore, we have it that the declared purpose and actual effect of an economic system is to reduce costs of production to the lowest possible proportion of output, we know at once that we are up against a purpose in production other than the natural purpose of satisfying the consuming needs of the working life of the world; because obviously such a reduction of costs of production—that is, of consuming rights distributed against output—to the lowest possible proportion of output, means that such an economic system operates so as to require the working life of mankind to produce more than it is permitted to consume.

And with that we begin to get daylight and understanding on the matter. For the conclusions to be drawn from this follow with mathematical certainty.

In such circumstances, there must be a surplus of production which passes out from the working life of the world for consumption elsewhere. If it were consumed within the working activities of the world's life, its consumption would be a cost of production, and costs of production would be equal to consuming rights over the whole output.

It follows that such a passing of wealth out of the working life of the world for consumption elsewhere *must* be in the nature of a levy of tribute. For all claims to participate in consumption by any sort of engagement in the human activities applied to natural resources by which the whole output is accounted for, come into the costs of production; everything which contributes in any way to production or to making consumption possible is accounted for in that; and outside that there is no possible or conceivable claim other than a claim to receive tribute.

It therefore further follows that the working life of the world cannot in such circumstances be the whole human life of the world. In the social order of such an economic system there must of necessity be—standing outside the working activities of mankind and contributing nothing to production or to making consumption possible—interests with recognized and established claims to receive the tribute.

And these interests must dominate the social order; because the dominant purpose of the economic system of which such a social order is the expression is the purpose of securing this tribute, and all the production and distribution of wealth must therefore be so governed as to serve that purpose. All the mechanism of such a social order, all its system of finance and costs and values, must be found on scrutiny to be designed and operated for the collection of the tribute; and all its social relationships will be found to be in conformity with this central purpose for which such a social order exists. Everything in the social order will be found to be shaped to the ends and subject to the purposes of tribute collection. And all this follows in the strictest sequence from the fact that keeping the costs of production as far as possible below output is the purpose which an economic system seeks to achieve in production. It is, indeed, nothing but an unfolded statement of what that purpose is.

And with that the meaning of "costs of production," which is such an insoluble puzzle from the natural view of production as human activity for the satisfaction of human needs, becomes clear as crystal. It expresses exactly what the sustenance of the working life of the world is to the governing tribute-receiving interests, to whom the consumption permitted to the working life of the world quite naturally figures as a reduction of the surplus available for tribute; and therefore from the point of view of their ownership, which is the point of view of our system of economics, a cost of production in the true sense of "cost"; something of which they are deprived in order to get the fresh production for profit which could not be forthcoming unless the working life of the world had its sustenance permitted to it.

What else becomes crystal clear is the meaning of

that immense conflict in our civilization, that straining of antagonistic purposes against one another in human affairs of which we have been conscious all through this enquiry, the sense of which conflict thrusts itself in the facts of life upon even the least perceptive mind. It stands revealed as a conflict of interests, the clash between the natural purpose of human activity in production as production for use and the insistence of our economic system that production shall be tribute-yielding production, production for profit.

When one speaks of this dominant and governing tribute-receiving interest as standing outside the whole working life of mankind, it is not suggested that it is an idle interest. On the contrary, it is extremely active and alert; engaged in the keenest possible way in its business of collecting tribute, a business involving vast activities with a world-wide network of finance and organization. That is only to say that it is not a passive reception of tribute, but a vigorously pursued business of levying it carried on through the active control of the economic system to that end; but none the less wholly outside the working life of mankind from which all production and all the possibilities of consumption flow. It obviously must be active; for a passive reception of tribute would imply some natural flow of consumable wealth away from the working life of mankind to which such wealth owes its whole existence. And that is an absurdity; the natural flow of produced wealth is into consumption within the working life of mankind, because the only natural reason for its production at all is the satisfaction of the consuming needs of that life. One would expect, therefore, to find a vast effort and organization necessary for diverting the flow of produced wealth away from its natural channels into this channel of tribute.

All this, as I have pointed out, is simply in the necessary implications of an economic system whose purpose it is to keep costs of production in the smallest proportion to output; and our task now is to test these deductions from the declared purpose of the system by the actual facts of its working, and see how far that test confirms them.

* * * * *

The basic fact in our economic system is the fact of private property in the natural resources of the world.

Certain elementary and axiomatic things in respect of such a form of property must be noted. As we have seen, there is no factor which enters into production or can enter into it other than human effort applied to natural resources; natural resources being the earth itself and all the store of varied materials, powers, and fertilities it contains which are capable of being shaped and fashioned and evoked by human effort to serve the needs of life. Debar human effort from access to natural resources and no production is possible, no making of anything. All human sustenance depends upon such access.

Ownership of the natural resources of the world is, therefore, ownership of all human opportunities to live; and carries with it the power of controlling the producing activities of mankind. With the establishment of this ownership, the right of the general community of mankind to shape and fashion and cultivate natural resources for the satisfaction of its need ceases, except on such terms as ownership chooses to attach to the right of access. For that is what ownership means. It is nothing other than the right to say, "This is mine; keep off except upon the terms on which I permit entry"; the "this is mine" here in question being all mankind's opportunity to live. And the terms are perfectly simple. In all the history of mankind under this system of ownership, access to the natural resources of the world has only been permitted to the working life of mankind on terms of service to the owner. The form of that service has varied from slavery to employment for hire; but the central fact in it, by which its essential character is revealed and defined, has always been that all the product belongs to the owner, less the "cost of production" represented by the maintenance of the slave or the hire of the worker. Such ownership, therefore, is the governing fact in the distributive system of any social order in which it exists, and is the power by which the producing activity of a community can be and is held to tribute.

It was under this system of ownership, with all its implications in the distribution of product and in the structure of social relationships, that the life of the world was carried on with comparative stability in the ages before power-production; and it remains, with all its implications in the distribution of product and in the structure of social relationships, the system of ownership, unchanged in its essential character, by which we are attempting to carry on the affairs of human life in a new world of power-production in which the possibilities of life have been enlarged and revolutionized into a new destiny for mankind.

The long-continued stability of this system of ownership as the governing fact in the social order through many centuries in the pre-power age of the world's history suggests that it was serving a purpose sufficiently worth serving to enlist for its survival a balance of power in the general force of life; that unconscious general urge of human tendencies which in any age is the deeper movement of life on which the conscious decisions men make on the surface of things are carried along. Without some such functioning effectiveness beyond the mere subjection of the general life to its privileges, no system could remain through a vast period of history; it must be in some way serving other purposes related to the growth movement of civilization; and have some quality in it appropriate to general human affairs at that stage and in the then circumstances of life. If that functioning relationship to such purposes ceases, the balance of power in the general force of life ensuring the survival of the system is turned against it; signs of confusion and disconnection between the social order and the purposes of the general life begin to manifest themselves; and a period of instability ensues, worsening through recurring crises of confusion until the necessary changes in its social order enable the general life to feel a renewed connection between its purposes and the system by which its relationships are governed.

Does not the present condition of the world's affairs give evidence that we are passing through just such a period of confusion? If we get things into their proper historical perspective, such periods of confusion would seem to be inevitable whenever new factors changing the character of man's struggle with Nature for existence make their appearance. The economic arrangements of any organized human society are the human artifices for carrying on that struggle in the way that commends itself to the general force of life as being most effective in relation to the known natural conditions of the struggle. When, therefore, new factors in the conditions of the struggle itself first make their appearance, they come into an existing order stabilized to the conditions known and prevailing before their appearance; and they naturally pass into the channels of social usage then existing. If they are compatible, they are duly absorbed without discomfort or instability into the existing social usages. But if they are incompatible, the incompatibility only becomes apparent by the growing pressure of discomfort and instability which they create in a system unable to assimilate them to its usages. It is not possible for men to see in advance what the nature of their impact upon existing social structures will be. That is all unknown and unsuspected, and can only reveal itself by experience. Such new forces in the natural facts of life cannot therefore come direct into a social order prepared for their reception; they can only create a social order fitted to them by such a pressure of discomfort and instability within the old order as will set a balance of power in the forces of life moving for new adjustments.

The Industrial Revolution—which is simply the substitution of gigantic non-human forces for our puny human physical powers as the energy of production and the measure of output available for human satisfactions —has completely altered both the character and the conditions of the struggle in which man has to engage with Nature for the sustenance of life. It has altered its character from the old indignity of harsh toil to mastery and command, and its conditions from meagreness to abundance. But it was inevitable at the outset that these new forces should pass into the existing usage, and be taken up on the lines of the established feudal tradition of appropriation by private ownership. They simply dropped into place as a new endowment for ownership, a new instrument for collecting tribute on a larger scale than before, in accordance with the established order of things; nobody thinking about it otherwise; everybody taking it for granted, by the inertia of old usage and immemorial class ideas, that these new things would be absorbed automatically into the old feudal master-and-serf structure of society without changing anything in the essential social relationships or class categories of men.

From the beginning of this thrust of the new powers into the system of feudal relationships of a social order based on human drudgery, all the signs of discomfort and instability indicative of a system whose arrangements have been thrown out of adjustment have multiplied upon us. The disconnection between the social order and the purposes to which the general life is urged by such a change in the conditions under which the human struggle with nature for sustenance is carried on, has been manifest in a growing confusion. What is now happening, on a world-wide scale and with growing urgency, is that this fundamental change which science has made in the basic life conditions of mankind is revealing itself, in one swift development after another, as incompatible with the old master-and-serf structure of society. The new powers are too great, too explosive in their reactions upon the old social relationships and the old limited purposes men saw in life, to be controlled and applied to life for the narrow purposes of a class society. Their immense productivity gets out of hand for such purposes; it becomes overproduction, glut, congestion beyond the capacity of feudalism in ownership and differential class distribution to absorb; and throws us into trade depression after trade depression by sheer weight of accumulated goods which cannot be marketed for lack of the purchasing power which a class society necessarily fails to distribute to its serfs and hirelings; with all the wars of the modern world as incidents in the growing confusion.[1] Over a period, the outside markets

[1] "Peace? Why, my fellow-citizens, is there any man here or any woman—let me say, is there any child—who does not know that the seed of war in the modern world is industrial and commercial rivalry? The War was a commercial and industrial war. It was not a political war. The reason that the War we have just finished took place was that Germany was afraid her commercial rivals were going to get the better of her; and the reason why some

gave some easement; but the discomfort, manifest from the first, has now grown intolerable, and the instability has become a prevalent terror of insecurity not only for nations and individuals everywhere, but for the future of human civilization itself.

The unrests of the old world, dynastic troubles and the like, were on the surface. Underneath them the essential life of the world, peasant production and the service of human needs according to the settled habits and relationships of an established order of things, remained stable. Masters fought and snatched power from one another; but the system of life was untouched by all that, because the natural conditions governing these fundamental things remained unchanged. But the unrest in the world to-day is in these deeper things. In all the turmoil of strikes, lock-outs, unemployment, labour troubles and trade convulsions, overproduction, bankruptcies, the struggle for markets, international conflicts, armaments and the menace of war, what is involved is maladjustment in the economic life of the world. Already civilization has been dragged to the edge of the abyss in a world war which was only the confusion of trade rivalries in the scramble for outside markets come to a head; and all the conditions for its repetition are still fermenting in the life of the world in the surpluses of products which the private ownership of our

of the nations went into the War against Germany was that they thought Germany would get the commercial advantage of them. The seed of the jealousy, the seed of the deep-rooted hatred, was hot commercial and industrial rivalry." (President Wilson, speaking at St. Louis, September 1919.)

opportunities to live takes in tribute and cannot get absorbed into use and the healthy nourishment of mankind. The world war has so far been its worst paroxysm of indigestion. And there is a certain appropriate symbolism in the fact that the next one will, according to all prediction, be in the nature of a universal belching out of poisonous gases.

CHAPTER XII

Our system of ownership and distribution remains, then, the old system of feudalism essentially unchanged; private property in the resources of the world as the basis of a social order, with the master-and-serf social relationship as its necessary corollary. Stable for ages in a world of scant production limited by dependence on human drudgery, its continuance as the basis of the social order and the governing factor in human affairs in a new world of power-production has, as we see, given us an age of confusion and instability without precedent in history. Let us examine a little more closely the circumstances of its old stability, and note the conditions within which such a system was capable of serving human needs effectively enough to ensure such a stability of long survival.

Human life in the pre-science age was almost universally the village life of small self-contained peasant communities, restricted for all the purposes of a real common life and regular intercourse to little more than walking distances; a world in which for pretty well everybody anything beyond the radius of a few miles from his village was foreign and remote.

In such self-contained peasant communities men lived for immemorial ages, and the economy of production and distribution in such a world was a simple matter. For supplies as well as for intercourse the community was dependent on its own resources; and a season's failure of the crops over an area no larger than a county meant local famine. They lived on the corn of their own district, and the meat and milk from local pastures. The wool and linen for their clothing, leather for shoes and saddlery, timber and stone for their houses, clay for their pottery and wood for winter warmth, were their local supplies. The land and labour on the land and the craftsman's handling of the products from the land; beyond what was available from these they had nothing. Exchange of produce with the outside over any long distance was difficult and was a negligible fraction of their supplies. In respect of metals it was often necessary to go further afield, and metals were consequently in the sparest use. For the staple continuous needs of life they were wholly dependent upon their own production within a narrow area. And all on the meagre scale of human physical power as the energy of production and the measure of output. Forty pairs of boots in a week and one man's labour only needed in their production, would have been the wildest fairy tale to them.

It was in such a world that feudalism—the private ownership of the community's opportunities to live, the land and the natural resources to which human labour must have access if the community is to survive—stood for long ages as the basis of the social order. For though it was a world of scanty production, Nature is so bountiful to mankind in resources and fertilities that even under such conditions the labour of a man with only the most primitive tools to help him could produce a surplus beyond his own keep.

And the purpose of all such ownership since the world began has been to collect that surplus as tribute to the owner; for if you can get possession of a man's opportunities to live and debar his access to them except on terms of service to you, all that he produces is yours, less the cost of his keep out of it. Whatever the form of service may be, slavery or serfdom or wage-hire, the cost of the man's living still leaves the surplus; and ownership of his opportunities to live is the power of taking it as tribute.

But in the pre-science age the surplus was meagre. The whole output of a man's labour was meagre, and his maintenance absorbed a large proportion of it. As a modern economist would put it, the costs of production were high. If such a community had been a co-operative commonwealth, with a common duty of toiling at production and a common interest in the product, the hardest toil by everybody would not have provided more than a scant life for anyone. Such a communal life would have been a hard life, without intermission of toil, and with a very little surplus beyond bare maintenance coming of it if that surplus had been absorbed into general consumption. But the surplus which would have been scanty for each if generally distributed could make a life released from drudgery and with ampler satisfactions possible for a few if they had the power to collect it; the power which ownership of the general opportunities to live gave them. And it was in that release of a few to ampler satisfactions than the drudgery of the pre-power age could give to the general life that the master-and-serf structure of society had its justification.

For there are things in human life beyond bare toil, and it is with their development that the growth movement of civilization is concerned. And with this form of maintenance for a governing class, the emergence of a human culture beyond the bare animal toil of physical existence became possible. That it was a frankly master-and-serf relationship; that those who benefited by it had little or no notion of serving any such wider purpose in the growth of human civilization; that it gave opportunities for oppressions, bestial cruelties and the mere arrogance of mastery; that it is *per se* an essentially unjust relationship; all that is not to the point. What is true is that it was the means by which certain qualities in human life other than the qualities which could be evoked by universal drudgery were able to develop, and that without it the conditions for the emergence of any sort of human culture beyond animal toil could hardly have existed in the ages when Nature exacted from mankind the hardest and most continuous toil for a bare pittance. It was probably the only means by which the development of any human type other than the drudge could have taken place; and it was to the force of life driving in that direction that the feudal structure of society owed its long stability.

In the circumstances of such a world no such developments beyond the drudge type were possible in the general life. The conditions of the human struggle with nature for sustenance doomed the mass of mankind to drudgery; and these other qualities in the growth movement of civilization had to appear as class qualities or not at all; as governing qualities and class authority, with all the evils attaching to them which are congenital in class privilege. But they were none the less a line of human advance and growth; and their class limitation was inevitable because the hard natural conditions of human sustenance forbade the release of the general life.

The change in the basic conditions of the human struggle with Nature for sustenance has brought us to the end of all that. What is implicit in the new powers is the release of the general human life from Nature's old exaction of drudgery for a bare pittance. They have removed the limitations which confined the cultural life of the race to a small class enclosure. That is their necessary impact on human affairs. They cannot be used to any other end without confusion and upheaval. If they are not permitted, according to their nature, to effect that release as a release into an enriched and enlarged leisure for men, a release for general human culture, none the less they do effect the release and it becomes our problem of resourceless unemployment. If they are not permitted, according to their nature, to provide plenty for all, none the less they do provide plentifully, and it becomes our problem of overproduction and the occasion of the wars by which the world is devastated in our scramble for markets into which to unload our unmanageable surpluses. They cannot be used for the narrow purposes of a class society without disaster; and our present confusions are simply the evidence of the helplessness of a class structure of society against them. That class structure, which was once the protective enclosure for such cultural growth as was possible in an age of scanty production, has become an obstruction to the wider human development implicit in the new powers; and its working arrangements are breaking down in every direction under the pressure of the new forces now demanding a new order of life in which to expand and function according to their nature.

* * * * *

The rationale of the thing is clear enough. What remains is to examine the actual working arrangement by which our system of private ownership of the world's opportunities to live has attempted to handle the new powers for the old class purpose of tribute collection, and see why they necessarily break down into confusion.

It has not been possible to collect the tribute in the old simple way. In the old peasant life of the world its collection was the simplest matter for the owner. For the most part, the produce of the human service which had to be rendered to him because of his ownership of everybody's opportunity to live was actual produce for direct use and consumption; delivered in kind into his barns and storehouses; in corn and wool and wood and whatever other supplies the locality yielded, and in many forms of direct obligatory service in the grinding of the corn and the delivery of the dues of the estate to the owner. He, like the peasant, lived mainly upon the produce of the estate, and took his toll for direct and immediate consumption; bartering an excess of any product either with neighbouring estates for other products in which his own estate was not so fruitful, or occasionally through the merchant who, in the most accessible market-town, represented in that infancy of the world's commerce the wider exchanges of sea-borne cargoes, mostly concerned with the silks and flounces of life. But all such outside exchanges were fractional in proportion to the staple things of life. The tribute in the main was local produce for direct consumption; marketing and exchanging hardly entered into it; and in that age of human drudgery production was so small that the surplus over and above the maintenance of the working life of the community was easily absorbed into direct consumption by the lord and the retinues he gathered round him for his personal service and the enforcement of his will. His retinues and his scale of living, the extent to which he was able to withdraw men from production and attach them to his band of retainers, either for fighting service or personal attendance on his wants or for the mere aggrandizement of his position, depended on the surplus available after the maintenance of the community's working life was provided for.

But to collect tribute from the output of power-production is a very different and much more complicated thing. The conditions under which the working life of the race keeps up its replenishment for consumption by fresh production have been completely altered. In pre-science production, human effort applied to natural resources resulted directly in things ready for use and consumption. The making of tools and equipment which were not themselves for actual consumption, but for assisting in the creation of final products, was a small and practically negligible proportion of the human activity needed for human maintenance. Hence the owner, coming into possession of the product in the natural sequence to his ownership of the community's opportunities to produce it, achieved his tribute-collecting purpose at first hand, in things he could eat and wear and use for his personal satisfactions.

Ownership in a world of power-production cannot do that. Human labour, while it has been superseded by non-human powers as the energy of production and the measure of output, still remains in its application to natural resources the sole creator of all wealth. But it is no longer the labour of an individual or a group of individuals producing direct from natural resources things which pass directly into use. It is labour mainly expended on evoking the new powers, and preparing the machinery and equipment and materials for them.

All such labour is, of course, related ultimately to some final product for use and consumption, and would be useless to mankind except in relation to such final products. But it is a relationship to *deferred* final products, in many cases to remotely deferred final products, the very nature of which is unknown to those engaged in these preparatory phases of our general effort for the replenishment of the world's supplies. The coal which a population of miners spend their lives in extracting from the earth in Durham may finally appear as a utility product in any commodity in any part of the world. It may take its final form as a usable product in giving you a railway journey, or it may pass through blast furnaces for the smelting of metals for the making of machines, and finally appear in human use as the boots you wear or any other output of the machine.

The general human activity for the renewal of the world's supplies now takes this form of preparing the way for the other than human energies of power-production. Power has to be generated, machines constructed; a world-wide collection of raw materials has to be made, and the materials when collected have to be passed through whole series of processes in preparation for final utility. Under the old pre-science methods of human effort, the small community of people living in a village and its immediate neighbourhood had to produce all the supplies for all their purposes of life, food and clothing and shelter, and all the utensils of living. Under power-producing conditions the life of whole districts may be given over to one specialized phase of producing something which in itself is of no use whatever to anybody until it has been passed on through a whole series of other processes on its way to final utilities. The flow of products replenishing the world's supplies for actual use and consumption is the resultant of all the human effort expended in these thousandfold antecedent activities. In such final production every scrap of raw material, every bit of every machine, every pound of power pressure, is only the terminal point of long lines of human activity applied to natural resources, so spread out over the whole world that it is almost impossible to trace any finished commodity back to all its sources.

Look at the simplest final product of this power system by which human wants are now supplied. What, for example, has gone to the making of the pen with which I am writing? The metal, with all the processes of ore-mining and transport and smelting; the machinery at every stage of each of these processes, each part of which has had to be prepared along the same lines; the coal for furnaces; the generation of power, again with long antecedents in all its mechanism; the buildings for the accommodation of power plants; all these and many other human activities going back and back along a thousand lines to raw materials extracted from nature. With every word I write, I am using up the final product of a world-wide ramification of human effort applied to natural resources in preparation for the final product.

The stream of final products passing at any moment into distribution for use and consumption is, therefore, the result of a new form which power-production has given to the general human effort for the replenishment of the world's supplies. In that new form, the production of final utilities, considered as a separate thing in itself, is only a fractional part of the human energy involved; the great and growing part of that energy—growing in proportion as power-production supersedes human drudgery—being devoted to preparation and equipment for final utility.

Now consider the bearing of this upon the procedure by which ownership collects its tribute from the working life of the world. The original procedure was, as we have seen, very simple. The ownership of natural resources is the ownership of the community's opportunities to live, since human life can only get sustenance by human effort applied to natural resources. Ownership of natural resources is therefore the power of compelling that human effort to take the form of service to the owner as a condition of access to the opportunity to live; and the terms of such service always are that the product belongs to the owner, who thus takes as tribute the surplus left of that product after allowing maintenance out of it to the human service so engaged. This maintenance must be made because the owner would get no service and no tribute if human beings were not kept alive to render it. It is "the cost of production"; and the central insistence of ownership economics is always that the cost of production must be kept down. If "costs of production"—i.e. the working life of the community—ate up all the produce, there would be no tribute, no surplus, no "profits" in ownership.

Neither in the manner nor the scale of its output does power-production lend itself to the purposes of a social order based on private ownership of the community's opportunities to live. In the scale of its output, the economy of such a social order is so hopelessly incompetent to carry power-production that it breaks down into what has now become a general world confusion under its weight. All its crises are crises of what it calls "overproduction," in which its arrangements crumple up under an output which is only a fraction of what power-production could give us and enormously below the human needs of the world's people. But it is with the manner of output under power-production that we are concerned at this point. It has, as we have just seen, made the production of supplies in final consumable form the team-work, not of a local community, but of the whole working life of vast populations expending their effort on intermediate processes in such a way that, although the activity of these populations as a whole is productively related to final utilities, their local and sectional activities are related to products of no consumable utility in themselves.

While at any given moment the flow of final products ready for use which this power-production method of output gives us is far greater than the world has ever known before, the human effort in production is no longer concentrated as it once was on those final products at their point of direct output. At any given moment the general human effort being expended on production is scattered widely over a great range of intermediate processes, and not applied at the point of final output. The enormously increased flow of such final output, with a steadily diminishing proportion of the total human effort in production engaged upon it at that point is, of course, due to the supersession of human labour as the measure of output.

Now, these preparatory and intermediate stages of production are all subject to a great multiplicity of separate ownerships. Each of them, in their almost endless ramifications, instead of being regarded as a part of the unified general human effort to replenish the world's supplies, is a separate business run for profit, a unit of ownership within which the owners have to collect their own separate tribute. Ownership in all these units functions in the normal way in which ownership of the community's opportunities to live is intended to function; the only way in which it can function. That is to say, it makes service in production service to the owner, and gives him possession of the product less the maintenance of the working human life engaged in the service.

But it is no longer a product on which either ownership or the working human life engaged in producing it can live by direct use and consumption. Over the wide range of our activities, when they are split up in that way into separate sectional ownerships, the product under power-producing conditions is an intermediate product, a thing or a part only of a thing of not the slightest use in itself to anybody in the world, a thing only intended for carrying on into further processes in the general effort of preparing for deferred final products. No actual human satisfactions can be got out of it.

And at the end of the process, when the final products themselves are the output, the same thing happens. What we have under power-producing conditions is not the little working community of a village with the economy of its life isolated by a world lack of transport, and producing in a simple and scanty way for all its own requirements; but communities of specialized workers whose output, even when it is a final product for use and consumption, does not provide for their living. What the owner gets is a mass of goods of one sort of no more use either to him or to his community of workers for their own personal satisfactions than intermediate products would be. They can no more live on 100,000 pairs of boots all ready for use than they could on 10,000 tons of steel intended for further industrial handling or on the square mile of floor-boards which came as intermediate products into the building of their factory. The owner gets the product, as the purpose of his ownership is that he should get it; but his actual tribute—his power of consuming for his own satisfactions—is locked up in the product and remains unavailable for his use in that form.

Clearly, since human life is continuous consumption, there must be some way of releasing both the owner's tribute and the maintenance of his workers from this lock-up in non-consumable products. All through the vast intricacy of the intermediate process, owners and workers have been living, and not upon nothing, although the division of the actual product between them in consumable form has not been possible. The division and their current sustenance in relation to it has been going on all the time; and in strict accordance with the law of ownership; maintenance to the working life engaged in producing the supplies and the surplus to ownership. To everybody concerned consuming rights have been distributed equivalent to what they would have had if the product itself had been in direct consumption amongst them; but they have been consuming rights in respect of the current flow of supplies.

That distribution has been through the monetary system—that great human convenience by which, through a common token of value, particular goods can be exchanged for general purchasing power instead of having to be clumsily exchanged for other particular goods in barter. And with that we come to the finance of our system of ownership and the enormous expansions, elaborations, and devices in connection with the monetary system which the linking up of power-production with such an ownership system has made necessary to serve the purposes of ownership economics. We pass from the realities of production and distribution as the handling of actual things into that region where the owner becomes the financer of production, human life engaged in production becomes labour costs, and commodities are no longer regarded as things produced for the satisfaction of human needs but as carriers of financial values; so that one does not say of them, "I have 10,000 pairs of boots ready for use," but "I have £1,000 worth of stock I want to clear."

*   *   *   *   *

But before passing on to that next and final stage of our examination of the arrangements by which the system of private ownership of the world's opportunities to live attempts to collect its tribute in a world of power-production, and why it necessarily comes to confusion and drags the whole life of the world into conflict and disorder, there is one point which needs to be emphasized in connection with these methods of output under power-production.

While the fact that so much of our activity is related to deferred final products through a long series of intermediate products does not take that activity in the least degree out of *productive* relation to the final products, quite clearly it does take it completely out of *consuming* relation to them. The life of the groups of people who, in this vast co-operation, are engaged on intermediate processes is not held up until some particular final product comes in due sequence from their special activity. The particular final products to which their part in the general human effort for renewal of supplies is contributing will on completion flow into the general stream for distribution into use; meanwhile their sustenance is in the general flow of final products already in process of distribution from the continuous activities of the working life of the world in which they are participating.

For the law of life and of human survival is immediate and continuous consumption accompanied by continuous provision for future consumption. In relation to sustenance, Nature knows nothing about deferred final products. The association between such deferred final products and human sustenance is the fantastic invention of our ownership-economics seeking to justify the tribute taken by ownership on the ground that the working life of the world has its sustenance advanced to it pending the appearance of final products. In actual fact, of course, nothing is advanced. Nothing can be advanced from to-morrow's sustenance for to-day's consumption. In the scheme of nature and the world of real things, consuming rights for all life are and must be always related to the immediate flow of consumable wealth, and not to what will come into flow next week. Consumption to-day in the natural order of things is not dependent on supplies being forthcoming next week; on the contrary, the existence of supplies for our survival next week depends absolutely on consumption to-day. As we shall see in a little, the finance of ownership in relationship to final products and the financial values locked up in them compels it, in its economic theorizing, to turn this obvious truism upside down; but it is none the less a truism in the world of sane realities.

Consumption never is and never can be in anticipation of product from the activities of the moment. It is the fulfilment of the purpose of past production. All products are deferred products, future provision; all harvests must be sown and allowed to ripen. In the old activities of the world the harvest of human effort was, on its ripening, almost wholly a harvest of directly consumable things. The new method by which the life of the world is served, while it has not really broken the relation which exists between all human effort and produce ultimately for direct use, has linked much of our activity to the ingathering of harvests which are not in themselves consumable, to the making of the apparatus of further making and of intermediate things. Production has in this way become more complex in detail; but in the fundamental service to life of a sustained and unbroken flow of consumption and replacement going on inseparably together its wide range of intermediate processes makes no difference whatever; and indeed could make no difference, because that is the flow of human life itself.

What its wide range of intermediate processes, disconnected in the life and work and output of vast populations from any immediate usable product, has done is surely to make clearer than ever the natural association of consuming rights, not with the product that will ultimately come of the work being done at the moment, but with the product of work previously completed and already available; makes it clearer than ever by reason of the remoteness of any such final product from the preparatory and equipment effort in which the mass of the working life of the community is always engaged at any given moment under power-producing conditions. Production is in all this a communal process; not only communal in respect of the activities of the moment, but communal in the continuity of life, yesterday and to-day and to-morrow. The obvious dependence of human life in such circumstances is upon the general flow of final products available at the moment; and all consuming rights would be related to that in any system of distributive economics in harmony with the facts of life. With planned production for use and a distribution related to human needs, the enormous increase in human satisfactions which the new powers make possible could be passed on into human life without any difficulty apparent to a sane mind concerned with the reality of things. All the activities of such production and distribution would seem to be capable of smooth and effective organization for human use in any world of ordinary intelligent and reasoning people.

CHAPTER XIII

Although it is necessary at the point we have now reached to speak in terms of the finance of the system, it is essential to clear understanding that we should constantly relate the finance procedure to the actual fact which the finance procedure implies in the real events of human life. For we have now got to the crux of the whole matter; and if we are to see clearly the reasons for the failure of our present system of ownership-economics and the confusions into which it throws the life of the world, and how these confusions do not arise merely by errors of judgment or avoidable mistakes made in operating it, but fatally and inevitably in the nature of the system itself, it is vitally necessary that we should see the facts as facts in human life, related to actual production and distribution in the service of human life, and not merely as finance procedure quoting the laws of its own working as an inexorable justification of whatever consequences may follow in human life. That is what every reference you hear to "the inexorable laws of political economy" amounts to. The things for which justification is attempted by showing in this way that the finance of our present economics works to such ends by the law of its nature, and artlessly assuming that the laws of its nature are the natural laws of human life instead of the artifices of a system of finance, are the very things from which the world is suffering; and this constant suggestion that the arrangements of a finance system are a code of inexorable laws to which the facts of human life must conform is the absurdity against which we have to keep our minds on guard when we begin to talk of markets, prices, costs, capitalization and financial values instead of human needs and the human effort to keep them supplied from the natural resources of the earth. The finance phraseology is the language of production for ownership profit, the factual phraseology the language of production for use.

* * * * *

All production, as we have seen, is covered by a multiplicity of ownerships, in each of which the primary purpose of ownership is being served—the delivery of the product into possession of the owner.

But the product so delivered, whether it be a final or an immediate product, is not, under power-producing conditions, available for personal consumption by the owner who receives it. His tribute is locked up in the product, and only becomes available to him when he puts the goods on the market and exchanges them for money, that common standard of values by which goods of any sort can be exchanged, not cumbrously for other specified goods, but for general purchasing power.

Obviously there are two kinds of market. If the product is a final product, it will pass to a consumer for use in the satisfaction of a human need. This market for final products is the market in which everybody is a buyer; for the consumer is everybody, the owning class in a nation as well as the working life of a nation; and it is therefore in the distribution of final products in this market that the real distribution of wealth into maintenance consumption for the working life of the nation and the surplus for the owners becomes effective. This is where everybody gets served, and the class allocation which our system of ownership exists to bring about becomes a real allocation in actual human satisfactions.

If, however, as is the case over a great range of the ownership units in our producing system under power-production, the product is an intermediate product, the market is a market in which ownership only is concerned. Such products pass from one ownership to another for further human effort to be expended upon them within the sphere controlled by the ownership to which they are transferred; and with this market, therefore, the consumer as consumer is not concerned, and the working life of the community is not a buyer.

Let us remember, here and all through the argument, that in all this flow of products, final and intermediate, into the markets, nothing whatever enters and nothing in the natural order of things can ever enter other than human labour applied to natural resources.

What, then, are the conditions under which ownership brings its goods to the market? Quite evidently it is here in the market conditions that the secret of the incompetence of the economic system will be found; because every confusion into which it leads the world's life is a confusion of "overproduction" in which our economic arrangements break down under a volume of products scantily insufficient for the world's actual needs and far below our producing capacity; even so meagre a weight of supplies being beyond the effective purchasing power the markets can exercise. What are the prices which ownership has to recover from the markets? And how are the markets equipped with purchasing power for absorbing the products at those prices? This stream of products flowing into the market is in its aggregate the world's continuous effort, within such conditions as the economics of ownership permit, to keep the supplies for human life replenished. What are the conditions under which products flow in? What are the conditions under which it is permitted to any one to take supplies out? The supply, the price, the effective demand? These are the vital questions.

All products coming into the market have locked-up in them, as costs of production, all the payments that have had to be made in respect of their production during their progress from raw materials through all the intermediate stages down to their completion for use. When at any intermediate stage any of the intermediate products have changed ownership and come under further human effort in shaping them towards their final form, or providing the power and equipment for so shaping them, the owner taking them over at that stage takes over all the costs previously accumulated in them; and these accumulated costs with the profits of the last selling owner added are the price at which they are transferred at any such stage. What has to be recovered in prices from the final consumer with whose purchase of it the product passes out of the producing system into final use is the sum of all these costs, again with the final seller's profit added.

These costs, in the first place, include all the cost of maintenance of all the human effort expended throughout every phase of the work. That has been distributed in money payments as wages and salaries; and since nothing whatever has entered into the making of anything in the whole process other than this human effort applied to natural resources, this is the only real cost. But in addition to this actual cost incurred there have been charges imposed, the levy of the tribute to ownership. At every intermediate stage at which a change of ownership has taken place, there has been the payment of the last selling owner's profit; and the completed products, ready for marketing by the final owner, are the carriers of financial values representing all these charges by and disbursements to intermediate ownerships as well as the labour costs. These charges may not always be actual payments of money. They may be and often are credit transactions based on the expectation of final marketing. But they are part of the charges to be recovered in prices from the consumer, with a still further charge in respect of the credit itself.

There are costs and charges beyond those incurred in production itself. All the finance side of the thing, devoted to checking and valuing and tracing the collection of the tribute, involves a special organization of accountancy and costings work. And finally there is the cost of the process of marketing itself. In the consumers' market for final products, producing businesses rarely sell direct to consumers. At the point of completion of such final products, a new ramification of ownership begins in the business of distribution, often through series of middlemen; and the effort of competition amongst producing firms to sell to these distributors requires a commercial organization in securing orders which is one of the sheer wastes of human effort to which the system subjects us; the mere effort of competition in selling, resonant throughout with blatant lying in advertisement. But one need not dwell upon that nor upon the sheer waste and parisitism of distribution through a superfluity of middlemen who contribute nothing to what is the necessary social service of distribution; for these are only blunders made in the working of the system and not in its inevitable consequences; blunders which could be remedied by better organization and are in many cases being so remedied. But so far as they continue to exist, they all add to the costs which have to be finally recovered from the consumer.

With all these costs and charges locked-up in them, final products make their appearance on the market. Now let us see how the market is equipped with purchasing power to absorb the goods at the prices necessary for the recovery of such costs and charges.

On the face of it the account should balance; because all the money distributed during the process of production to meet these costs and charges at once becomes purchasing power in the hands of those who receive it. The costs and charges are the sum of all payments made in wages, salaries, rewards for services of every kind, dividends, profits, rents, interest and credit charges; everything, in short, which has been disbursed; and assuming any sort of steadiness in the value of money, should therefore represent a general purchasing power pretty well equivalent to the prices which have to be recovered from the consumers' market.

But our whole problem is that things do not in fact work out at that equivalent. If they did there could be no problem of overproduction; for overproduction is nothing but the presence in the market of goods for which the market does not possess purchasing power. There never is in the home market of any power-producing nation an exercisable purchasing power equivalent to the prices which have to be recovered for its products. The whole scramble for outside markets is because of that; the wars of the modern world are incidents arising from it. And since, as we have just seen, there is, as a matter of strict accountancy, always a distribution of purchasing power precisely equivalent to the costs and charges determining the market price of products—the two things are indeed the same thing, two sides of the same shilling, the payment which is accounted as costs by the producing system being the receipt by the person to whom it is paid of purchasing power for use in the market as a consumer—there is here a direct contradiction between the facts as they appear in the financial system and the actual facts as they are in the events of life.

There are two reasons why the thing does not in

fact work out at the equivalent; why in fact the economy of ownership is fatally compelled by the law of its own nature to produce an unmarketable surplus.

In the first place, the second market has been left out of the reckoning; the market for intermediate products, which is not a consumers' market, but is confined to ownership. What is spent in this market is, in effect, the renewal and extension of the capitalization of production for further final products. Under an economic system which makes the capitalization of industry—its equipment and financing—the function and mode of living of a section of the population instead of a community function, all money spent in this market on equipment and intermediate products is money put into the ownership system by way of establishing a further claim to the ownership of further products; and it is a constant exhortation to owners that the incomes distributed to them in dividends and profits should be partly withheld from personal consumption and saved for this purpose of providing the capital equipment of ownership. To the extent to which this is done, there is a surplus of final products on the consumers' market for which no purchasing power is forthcoming, an unmarketable surplus.

As this is a point at which we touch the vital weakness of ownership-economics, let us examine it with the closest attention. For the fatal defect in the system is that it is compelled to produce an unmarketable surplus, and here is one of the secrets of that compulsion.

When an owner receives a payment of dividend or profit, he receives it as personal income. It comes from his ownership, but he receives it as his personal purchasing power in the consumers' market; receives it in his capacity as one of the general body of consumers. It is paid out of the producing system into the consuming system. In the finance of production, its payment is a cost which has to be carried to account for recovery from the consumers' market; but in the hands of the person to whom it is paid it is part of the equipment of the consumers' market with a sufficiency of purchasing power to enable that recovery to be effected in the prices paid by consumers; a purchasing power, as we have seen, equivalent to what has to be recovered in prices, balancing the market.

This recovery *can only be effected in the consumers' market for final products*. It cannot be effected in the market for intermediate and equipment products. That is not a consumers' market. All transactions there are within the ownership system. When an intermediate product is sold it passes, not into consumption, but into further ownership within the producing system for further handling in or equipment of production. The money passing at its sale is not paid from the consuming system to the producing system in recovery of costs; it is only the taking over by one owner from another of all the costs and charges which are locked up in the commodity at that stage; and they remain locked up in it, to be carried on, through however many such changes of ownership it may pass, until the completed products, carrying the accumulation of all such charges, pass into the consumers' market for the recovery of that total in prices.

All the costs and charges of all the intermediate stages of production are invariably carried forward through every such stage and on into final products, and are recoverable only by the marketing of final products in the consumers' market.

The owner receiving the payment at any of these transfers of intermediate products within the ownership market gets his profit released to him as personal income; such personal income, however, being part of the renewed equipment of the consumers' market with purchasing power of which the equivalent will appear in the prices of the final products resulting from the serial of production in respect of which the purchasing power is distributed.

Reinvestment from personal income, therefore, withdraws from the consumers' market purchasing power by which the market is equipped to meet the prices of one serial of production, and returns it unused into the producing system, where its expenditure on intermediate products and equipment becomes a disbursement to be accounted as costs carried into and recoverable from a further serial of production. Meanwhile the financial values contained in the final products of the previous serial, in whose costs and charges the reinvested income was originally distributed as purchasing power, have been a surplus of prices irrecoverable in a market in which that equivalent purchasing power has not been exercised.

All money which is spent on intermediate products appears, therefore, twice as costs in the finance of the producing system and enters twice into prices to be recovered from the consumers' market, but only makes one appearance in that market as the purchasing power by which the costs have to be recovered in prices. The central tribute-collecting purpose of the system, in short, involves it in a perpetual attempt to collect from the consumers' market what the necessities of its own continuance as ownership prevent from being there to collect.

Here then we have at least one of the sources of that unmarketable surplus which our present economic system is compelled to produce; the surplus which clogs its markets, drives it to its commercial adventures for outside markets, reproduces the same thing there as those markets are developed, and finally makes the confusion a world-wide threat of disaster to civilization in war and general breakdown.

The production of the unmarketable surplus is not an accidental defect in the working of our present ownership-economics. In this one cause of it we have just been examining it is quintessential in the system of ownership itself under power-producing conditions. For what power-production has done is to make the human effort by which life is provided with its supplies an effort devoted to vast equipments over long series of intermediate processes through which the new powers operate for the production of final utilities, instead of an effort producing final utilities at first hand. It therefore imposes upon our system of ownership, if it is to sustain itself as ownership, the need for these equipments towards final utilities; because it is only in final utilities that ownership can collect its tribute.

Ownership has to finance the equipment in order to perpetuate itself as ownership of the final products. All capitalization, therefore, is simply the establishment of title to ownership of final products from which tribute can be collected; and money devoted to financing the equipment comes into the economy of production as the measure by which the life of the community is subject to tribute to the owners of the means of the community's livelihood; a debt which must be paid by the consumer, who is everybody, and is as we have seen collected in prices. And these equipments and intermediate processes cannot be financed by private ownership in any other way than by not consuming a portion of the tribute-income which has been distributed as purchasing power in respect of previous final products already come to market.

The finance of production for ownership profit, therefore, requires on the one hand that every disbursement made by the producing system shall be reckoned into the prices to be collected from the market, and on the other hand has to divert from the market—as its only means of keeping its necessary equipment going—money distributed as purchasing power to make that collection possible.

This suicidal necessity does not arise from the need for the equipment itself, which is in the nature of power-production, but from the need of ownership to retain its control of production. It must finance the equipment to retain the ownership of final products.

The need for the equipment itself, separated from this endeavour of ownership to sustain itself as ownership, could of course be met in the simplest possible way by a socially planned production for use; because nothing enters into this equipment-production other than human effort applied to natural resources. It is all related to final products. It is the power-producing way of arriving at final products; the form which the unified human effort in any socially planned creation of our supplies has to take under power-producing conditions. But the finance of private ownership can only provide for the sustenance of its equipment by this absurd procedure of depriving the consumers' market of purchasing power, and breaks its own back with a surplus of unmarketable products as a result. Were it not for the incessant bankruptcies and liquidations, constantly jolting some of this incessant increment of capitalization out of the economy of things altogether, and thereby writing off a portion of the debt of the community to ownership, the whole thing would have gone to pieces long ago under its weight of capital expansion; which does not mean expansion of equipment for production, but expansion of the financial claims created against final products by this method of providing the equipment.

All this equipment-production is, in the actual facts of life, nothing but the normal working process by which the life of the world gets things for use and consumption under power-producing conditions. Its appearance in our ownership-economics as "capitalization" is the finance fiction. For since nothing whatever enters into actual equipment-production other than human effort applied to natural resources, the "capital" which has to be provided is and can be nothing but the bread and butter and clothing and other maintenance consumed by that labour during production; all of which comes from the stream of final products already in process of distribution, the flow of the world's wealth provided for no other purpose than to keep life going by continuous consumption associated with further production. "Capitalization" adds nothing whatever to it; and is merely the register of the fact that, instead of flowing normally into use and consumption by the working life of the world, it has been appropriated by ownership in tribute previously taken—the purpose of the whole system being precisely such appropriation of final products—and cannot, therefore, be consumed without permission of ownership. Capitalization expenditure, the "financing" of equipment-production, is merely the distribution of such permits. It stands for nothing whatever in the reality of things and presents no problem at all to any socially planned production and distribution of products. It is merely the title of ownership to tribute asserting itself over the flow of resources by which the world's life has to be maintained during further production.

* * * * *

There is another contributory reason for the unmarketable surplus.

The distribution of purchasing power is not a distribution to all consumers according to the flow of wealth available for consumption or the ratio of production to population. It is the unequal distribution prescribed by our system of ownership; maintenance allowances for the working life of the nation and the surplus to ownership.

When in the pre-science days the output was meagre, the maintenance of the working life of the community absorbed a high proportion of it. But under power-producing conditions the disparity between output and a mere sufficiency for maintenance is very great. The measure of our output is far and away beyond the old human-energy limit to production; and with every further development in power-production the surplus of output beyond maintenance grows greater and greater. But the distribution of purchasing power to the working life of the nation—which is the general mass of the population—remains a maintenance allowance distribution in wages according to cost of living; a distribution not in any way related to the ratio of production to population, but based on the comparatively static requirements of human bodies for nourishment and physical health. And this means that the consumers' market is equipped with purchasing power, not evenly over the whole population, but very sparsely in proportion to output over the general mass of people and in very great abundance to a few; and this grotesque maldistribution makes a good deal of such purchasing power as is distributed ineffective.

The distribution of purchasing power on a huge scale to a small proportion of a vast population does not and cannot make up the deficiency of the market resulting from a meagre scale of distribution to the general mass of the population; any more than a few oases can turn Sahara into a fertile land. In the pre-science age, when production was confined to the narrow limits of unaided human energy, the economics of ownership which we have inherited from those now remote times did not prevent the community from consuming its own product. Then, as now, it distributed, as its nature is, unequally; but the surplus which went to ownership when the maintenance of labour-service had been allowed for was consumable. But with a power-production output almost unimaginably greater per head of population than then, and the mass of the population still on maintenance rations, no such absorption is possible.

For there is, so far as the ordinary needs of life are concerned, a limit to possible personal consumption. No man can eat breakfast for a thousand. If a thousand people are going without eggs, it does not restore the equilibrium of the egg market to give one man purchasing power for a thousand eggs. He cannot do it; even twenty eggs at a sitting is the sort of meal only occasionally attempted by sportive and adventurous persons doing it for a wager. He cannot wear out more than a limited number of shoes, or, indeed, carry any of his physical satisfactions beyond repletion.

There are other and more expansible appetites and indulgences in comforts and luxuries; but when he has added all these to his consumption, he can go but a very little way towards making up for the deficient marketing powers of millions of other people. With the utmost scale of luxurious living on the ownership side, the inability of the general population to consume more than a fraction of what our output ratio to population would allot to them remains unbalanced by the ability of a few to consume to repletion.

The effect of this upon production is manifold. The purchasing power in the possession of the mass of the population, restricted in this meagre fashion, is insufficient to set power-production going beyond a fraction of its capacity. The nation is not permitted to provide for its own need. Practically the whole of the purchasing power of the general population is used up for sheer necessaries, with a small margin of the cheapest pleasures and gratifications without which life would be quite intolerable; and these are frequently only obtainable by cutting down expenditure on primary necessaries.

The lower margin of ownership incomes has also to be spent on primary necessaries; but when this requirement of life has been fully served expenditure in the upper margin of big incomes naturally exfoliates into luxury expenditure. To meet this kind of demand arising from the maldistribution of purchasing power much productive effort is diverted from necessary things which the general life requires but cannot purchase, to the luxury requirements for which a purchasing demand is forthcoming from ownership incomes. Hence a nation which leaves a large proportion of its children without a proper supply of warm clothing—enquire at any public elementary school and see—will be found to be applying a good deal of its labour and its materials to the provision of fur coats and wardrobes of fashionable frocks for ownership. Quite a charming and admirable purpose to which to apply effort and materials for the satisfaction of any section of the nation delighting in such things after the primary needs of the nation's life have been exhaustively served; but scarcely so admirable while hardly one in a hundred of the general mass of the child population has a really adequate supply, by any decent standard of adequacy, of good woollens for underwear during the winter.

With the growth of what is still only a very rudimentary social conscience in these matters, some attempt is now made by most civilized nations to correct the worst features of this maldistribution through the agency of social services; taking money by taxation from the upper ranges of large incomes and devoting it to such purposes as the provision of milk for nursing mothers, sustenance for unemployed persons, pensions for the aged, and so on. This, in effect, means transferring a little of the nation's labour and materials from the making of fashionable frocks and the other forms of luxury to which it would be devoted if left in the upper margin expenditure of large incomes and using it for the supply of common necessaries.

From the point of view of the national life regarded as a whole, this would obviously be neither a burden upon nor an addition to national resources, but only a slight correction of their maldistribution. But, as we shall shortly see, the economics of our present system drive ownership into a furious competitive struggle to collect its profits by selling products in the world's markets; and the cost of such social services, levied in rates and taxes, is a disbursement which has to be recovered in prices by the owners of producing businesses upon whom the levy is made. It adds to the cost of production; the cost of production being the standard of maintenance allowed to the working life of the nation. These social services are in fact an addition to the maintenance allowance which the ordinary working of the system permits to the general life of the nation; and the necessity for recovering in prices this addition to costs handicaps ownership in every market in which its wares have to compete with cheaper products into whose price such costs do not enter.

Any really substantial attempt to correct the maldistribution in this way would, therefore, deprive ownership of its competing power in the markets; and human life stands baulked of its escape from maldistribution and its resultant poverty along that line within the existing system. For it is a line which could not be followed to any great lengths without smashing the existing system by destroying its competitive effectiveness in its markets.

The idea that such an extension of social services carried to great lengths would so level up the distribution of consuming rights as to create a home market in compensation for the lost outside markets will not stand against examination. What that idea involves in practice is the elimination of the purposes and powers of ownership while still retaining its form; and no such equalization of consuming rights by their distribution outside the normal wages and payments for services is possible within the class structure of the existing economic system itself. It would be an attempt to create a new system of distribution directed to the elimination of class by the equalizing of consuming opportunities; and such a new system would demand its appropriate social structure in respect of ownership. Within the existing system, such social services cannot be more than eleemosynary provision for hard cases without challenging the ownership system itself, and involving a transfer to social agencies of the ownership and control of the community's opportunities to produce as a condition of the socially directed distribution of consumable resources. As a means, therefore, of compelling social action in regard to ownership itself, such large-scale extensions of social services for the distribution of consuming rights by other means than wages might be advocated, with all the problems attaching to such a procedure in relation to keeping the flow of wealth itself going; but inside our existing ownership-economy, not as a challenge to it, but as a method of distribution supposed to be conformable to the existing order, it will not stand examination.

But apart from all this maldistribution of purchasing power the method of providing for production by private ownership capitalization has, as we have seen, the inherent and congenital defect of creating an unmarketable surplus. Maldistribution still further disables the home market of any nation developed and equipped for power-production from absorbing its own products or their financial equivalents; so that whole districts of England are given over to the production of textiles for world-wide markets, while armies of English people have an insufficiency of shirts and use old newspapers for table linen. "Year by year," said Mr. Reginald McKenna in his address to the American Bankers' Association, "England produces more than she can either consume herself or exchange for the products of other nations." But the maldistribution, though it thus adds to the national disablement from absorbing what is produced, is the outcome rather than the root of the matter. Maldistributed as it is, a purchasing power equivalent to the aggregate of all prices for all products is, in fact, paid out from the producing system as income to consumers. While maldistribution prevents it from being effectively used, the ownership method of capitalization goes deeper and compels its disappearance from the consumers' market, leaving a surplus of irrecoverable prices locked up in unmarketable products.

This is the fatal and incurable flaw in our system of production for profit, by reason of which the financers of production in any power-producing nation are compelled to seek outside markets for that surplus, and take payment from such outside markets in some form other than products in exchange. And into the development of events in the outside markets it now remains for us to follow up our enquiry.

CHAPTER XIV

Let us be quite clear, to begin with, as to what it is that ownership, with this surplus on its hands, has to seek and find in the outside markets.

It is not simply the exchange of goods for goods. A proportion of the goods sold abroad is not surplus to the purchasing power possessed by the home market, but is sent abroad in the course of that real and beneficial trading by which products are exchanged for products for the sake of greater variety in the gratification of human tastes and desires. Instead of living exclusively within the monotony of its own native and climatic products, a nation can in this way of exchange enjoy the varied products of all lands and climates.

There is also the fact that in the nature of power-production its raw materials have to be gathered from a wide area, and it specializes the output of great populations to products which are not in themselves sustenance; products for which an exchange of food and raw materials must therefore be sought outside the producing area, and often from abroad. No problem arises or need arise about trade of this sort. It is all based upon, and cannot exceed, the purchasing power possessed by the home market; and goods equivalent to those sent out can therefore be brought back and the financial values locked up in them recovered by their sale in the home markets.

The problem is as to the excess of products *beyond the purchasing power of the home market.* Our economic system, as we have seen, is compelled to produce such a surplus; goods which, as Mr. McKenna points out, the producing nation can neither consume nor exchange for other products. Other products taken in exchange can no more be absorbed by the home market than the original home products could be; for an equivalent purchasing power is necessary for their absorption and the home market does not possess it. The financer of production would therefore be in precisely the same embarrassment with such equivalent goods on his hands as when he was compelled to seek an outside market for the original goods. The financial values which he has to collect by their sale would still remain locked up in commodities from which the purchasing power in the home market is unable to release them to him. What, therefore, he has to seek and find is not only an outside market, but a release of his locked-up financial values in some other form of payment than the return of financially equivalent goods.

Mr. McKenna, whose speeches as a rule show a much clearer discernment of the facts in human life which are hidden in a finance formula than is the case with most big bankers, falls into what must surely be obvious feebleness on this point. After pointing out to the American Bankers' Association the plain fact I have already quoted from him—that a developed power-producing country produces a surplus of goods which it can neither consume nor exchange for other goods—he went on to argue that such a country "could not obtain a market for this surplus unless by giving the purchaser a long credit." In this way, he added, "the factories and workshops are kept in employment, but it is a condition of their prosperity that a part of their output should be disposed of in this way."

It is surely self-evident that in such circumstances no suggestion of credit, whether long or short, meets the needs of the case at all. The surplus is a surplus definitely beyond the purchasing power of the nation to absorb. Nor is it an isolated surplus produced now and again, with periods of greater purchasing power in relation to output intervening, during which the surplus from the exceptional periods of overproduction can be absorbed. It is, as we have seen, in the essential nature of the finance of our existing ownership-economy that it always does and must produce this unmarketable surplus, whether in times of expanding or of depressed trade. If it goes on producing at all, the purchasing power available in its home market is, to the extent of its capital outlay on intermediate products and equipment during that production, less than what it has to collect in prices if it is to recover its costs; for all such outlay, as we have seen, while it appears in costs of production and therefore in prices, does not appear as purchasing power in the consumers' market for final products, where the costs have to be recovered in prices. And a nation thus habitually producing such a surplus by the unavoidable necessities of its own methods of financing production, cannot absorb the equivalent of its surplus by deferring its receipt of that equivalent from its outside markets any more than by claiming it in immediate payment. The thing goes a great deal deeper than any question of credit or deferred recovery of prices.

The facts themselves are perfectly clear as to the form in which payment for the surplus has to be taken. It has to be taken by investing it abroad in loans to and capitalization of the outside market countries; and the market which has to be found for the surplus is a market in such countries as require loans and capitalization. The payment has to be taken in "securities"; that is to say in certificates of new ownership set up in the market countries.

And this, in effect, means that the payment has to be left as a debt; because, as we have seen, all capitalization under our present system makes its appearance in the economy of the world in the form of a debt from the producing system to the financer of production—that is to say, from the working life of the community to ownership—by the creation of charges upon production and claims to final products. Taken in this way, therefore, the payment for surplus product sold abroad is the creation of charges upon the produce of the outside countries, to which the capitalization and the loans constitute a title; precisely the same title to tribute as our feudal economics of ownership stand for everywhere.

In short, the system which creates the difficulty of the overproduced surplus has to be extended to the market country into which the surplus goes; and a process of capitalized development set going by which the market country is carried rapidly towards industrialization and itself becomes an equipped producing country with an unmarketable surplus of its own, for which in turn it has to seek an outlet.

Ordinary trade for exchange of products can be carried on between fully-developed countries; but for the disposal of this overproduced surplus which is at the root of the trouble—the surplus which exceeds the available purchasing power of the producer nation—the main outlet must be in those areas of the world still waiting for development; for these are the only areas in which the financer of production can collect the payment for the surplus in the only form in which, as we have seen, he is able to receive it. The already developed countries present but small opportunities for the collection of payment in that form; they have their own overproduced surplus to get rid of, and their difficulties in getting rid of it would only be increased if the purchasing power in their own home market, already insufficient to absorb the surplus, were permitted to be sponged up by making payments from it for the imported surplus of other countries.

It is, therefore, upon the capture of the undeveloped or less developed areas of the world for market purposes that competition between the already developed countries becomes fiercer and fiercer. In large measure the goods poured in upon them from the surpluses of the replete countries take the form of equipment-goods for the development of the country; rails and engines for new railways, girders for bridges, the equipment of new harbours, material required for water-supply, lighting, local transport and other services for its developing towns, generating plant for power; and, in a rapidly increasing ratio as the country passes from primary equipment to industrial development, all the varied machinery and apparatus for production.

There comes a stage in this development when the market country begins to show a tendency to import a less proportion of manufactured goods and a greater proportion of raw materials for its own growing industries; tariffs against the further inflow of manufactured goods begin to be levied; and so the country passes into the array of the competing countries, fighting for outside markets of its own as a vent for surplus. The market countries only serve their turn as markets for the surplus of the replete and fully developed countries for the period until they too reach this stage of becoming equipped competitors in the world scramble.

As a constantly widening area of the world becomes thus developed, the struggle for remaining outside markets naturally grows more and more desperate. The area of such markets diminishes, while the number of competitors for them increases. The quarrels and conflicts of nations and Governments are almost entirely concerned with this struggle; it was the over-produced surplus of our economic system seeking its outlet that dug the graves and provided the corpses of millions of the world's youth in 1914–1918. Without outside markets our economic system would die of congestion. It must fight for them to the death with savage intensity; and when it gets them it is compelled, always by the fatal pressure of the over-produced surplus which the finance of its own capitalization makes unavoidable, to equip every customer nation for rivalry in production and a further intensification of the struggle.

The concrete facts of the world's present position illustrate all this. The replete nation by this process becomes a creditor nation. Great Britain, for example, under the pressure of having to find outside markets for the surplus for which it is unable to take equivalent goods back for British consumption, has accumulated such vast investments in the development of less fully equipped countries that the world to-day owes a yearly interest payment of about £300 millions to British financers; and that is only one national item in a huge indebtedness of the world's producing life to the finance interests; indebtedness created by the disposal of the unmarketable home surpluses of the replete countries in outside markets from which payment for it can only be taken in this form of establishing titles to permanent charges and rights of collecting tribute from the world's producing system.

The receipt of this annual tribute raises another set of difficulties and problems for the finance of ownership. In what form can it be received? And how used?

The economic prohibition against taking goods in exchange for the surplus originally sent out—the prohibition set up by the fact that such goods or their equivalents are surplus to the purchasing power available in the home market—does not, of course, operate against the receipt of this tribute in commodities. For it is tribute received as income, as purchasing power in the consumers' market against the output of the producing system of the nation paying the tribute. The financial values locked up in the goods originally sent out have been released to the financer of their production; released in the form of an established title to receive a consumers' income from the output of the outside producing system. To the extent to which such consumers' purchasing power is distributed from outside into any country to the holders of foreign investments, equivalent goods can come in and be marketed by the exercise of that purchasing power—which is in effect only a certificate of title to the goods—independent altogether of the distribution of consuming rights in respect of home production.

But consider what happens if it is so received. There is nothing in the essentials of our economic system to prevent a section of a nation, or a whole nation for that matter, from living on tribute in this way by the importation of products from outside. But obviously a nation living entirely on tribute so rendered would be a nation in which the need for employment in production would cease. The only employment necessary in such a case would be in the distributive handling of the imported goods and, so far as any helot class was available, in personal service to the receivers of the tribute. And what would thus be comprehensively the case with a nation living wholly on tribute from outside is proportionately the case to the degree in which any section of a nation lives in the same way. To that degree the life of the nation dispenses with home production; with the result that either such home production is correspondingly decreased or the surplus of its products unmarketable in the home market is increased.

The tribute therefore cannot be received in goods without seriously damaging the interests of the financers of production and the security of employment for the working life of the nation into whose consuming economy the goods are admitted. Even in a Free Trade country like Great Britain not half of the annual tribute of about £300 millions on foreign investments is received in goods; while tariff countries like the United States set themselves resolutely, in the interests of production within their own borders, to prevent its receipt in that form at all; so resolutely as even to bar the re-entry of their own goods once they have been sent out. As for example when at the close of the war a great number of transport vehicles were left in the war area by the United States army, and a prohibition duty of 90 per cent put upon their reimportation to America.

In that case how then is it received? For the United States or any other producing country walled round with tariffs to prevent its receipt in goods, none the less goes on and must go on producing its home-unmarketable surplus for which it has incessantly to find an outside market and receive payment by buying securities and making investments abroad and thereby establishing title to annual tribute. The individual holder of foreign investments in such a tariff country receives his certificate of payment, and changes it through his bank into its equivalent of purchasing power within the finance of his own country's consuming system. It becomes in that way a claim on his own country's goods for consumption; and the banks, through the international arrangements for making such settlements, have to collect something real on it from the country of its origin; something equivalent to the consumption of home goods for which it has become the warrant. What is so collected? Not goods; that is prohibited. What then?

Nothing but its renewed reinvestment abroad; the creation of a further title to further increments of tribute.

There is, or there was thought to be until a year or so ago, another practicable alternative. The finance arrangements of the system include the establishment of gold as an international monetary standard and measure of values. Why not, therefore, receive it in gold?

With the consequences of trying to receive it in that way beyond the merest margin and settlement of balances, the whole world should by this time be very thoroughly acquainted. Two of the main creditor nations of the world—the United States and France—have been receiving it very largely in that form; with the result that, of the £2,233 millions of gold held throughout the world by the central banks of the 45 principal nations—held with the main intention of regulating the "international exchange" as the flow of this tribute from one country to another is humorously described by the financial interests that live by it—no less than £1,346 millions is at the moment buried in the vaults of the central banks of America and France; substantially more than half. This has made gold so scarce and so scrambled for amongst the debtor communities of the world thrown back in this way on having to meet their obligations in gold, that its value against goods rises higher and higher, and a constantly increasing volume of real products has to be paid for it. In other words, the price of all commodities has crashed down catastrophically; and the producing system of the world has therefore to allot much more of its actual products to the settlement of all the debts and charges held against it by the finance system.

Australia is one of the most illuminating examples of this. The financial return for the Australian wool crop in 1928, expressed in gold terms, was £66 millions. For what was an identical crop in volume in 1930 the financial value received was £36 millions; nearly twice as much wool for every gold unit. But the debt claim on the Australian producing system by the financial system of the world has to be paid by the gold measurement and not by wool measurement; and the Australian producing system has therefore to be deprived of twice as much actual produce as before in order to meet these claims; leaving it with an enormously reduced supply of actual produce for standard of living purposes for the human life of Australia. That is an outstanding illustration; but everywhere throughout the world production has been checked, and human suffering through bankruptcy and unemployment has risen to a climax in the worst depression in economic history.

That is what has come of the attempt on the part of the financial interests in one or two of the principal creditor nations to collect a substantial portion of the tribute in gold. Gold as a measure of values and ultimate exchange against the vast producing powers of the world is a sufficiently childish absurdity even were it handled by the money-powers controlling the banking system with the utmost precaution against its obvious dangers and inadequacy; but when it comes to the use of gold for actual bulk debt settlements the ludicrous insufficiency of all the available supplies of the metal against the vast indebtedness of the world to the finance system makes it grotesque. How grotesque may be judged by the fact that the tribute debt which now has to be paid each year to holders of foreign investments in the United States alone amounts to about four times the whole world's annual production of gold.

Since therefore the tribute cannot be received in products without injuring production and employment in every country to which it goes in that form, and cannot be collected in gold without the catastrophic effect on prices manifest in the facts of 1930, nothing remains but the old way of reinvesting it. The original investment upon unloading into the outside market the overproduced surplus for which no other payment was receivable, the tribute from the original investment, the tribute from the investment of the tribute, and so on in progression, all come into the same category; constant extensions of title to ownership and still further tribute throughout the world.

The economic history of the world since the coming of power-production has been the movement of events along this line of development. It has been a development complex enough in its detailed confusions—in the internal class conflicts to which it has given rise in the social order of every nation and the external conflicts and rivalries between nations threatening civilization itself with disaster—but perfectly simple in the essential sequence with which the results of attempting to handle power-production for profit and the purposes of class-ownership instead of for plentiful use in the life of the world have manifested themselves. The compulsion, unavoidable in the purposes and methods of our system of ownership, to produce a home-unmarketable surplus; the consequent necessity of going outside for markets; the inability to collect payment from those markets except by developing and equipping them for similar production on their own account; the consequent growth of new rivalries, each stimulated by the compulsion of its own unmarketable surplus; and so, slowly at first but at a rapidly increasing pace as the surpluses multiply and the rivalries grow to desperation, the constant extension of the world area within which purchasing power is unable to absorb output, and the dwindling of the outside area into which ownership can throw the surplus for realization: to set down this sequence of events is simply to note the main course of economic history during the period in which the new powers have been cramped down into the mere appurtenances of surviving feudal rights of ownership over the world's life. And it has brought us to the point at which ownership not only starves the general life of what might flow into it from the planned use of these powers of plenty for all mankind, but cannot even effectively collect its own claims to tribute in respect of the surplus; the surplus beyond what the general life is permitted to consume, which it is the sole purpose of the whole system of ownership to secure for itself.

The facts do not seem to be in dispute; they are indeed so obvious as to be indisputable. It is the helpless futility of the suggestions made for dealing with them that is amazing. Thus Mr. McKenna, as we have seen, agreeing that the system compels a nation to produce what it is neither permitted to consume itself nor can exchange for other products, suggests "long credits"! President Hoover also describes the facts with perfect clearness. "We have," he says, "an equipment and a skill in production that yields us a surplus of commodities for export beyond any compensation we can usefully take by way of imported commodities. There is only one remedy, and that is by the systematic permanent investment of our surplus in productive works abroad. We thus reduce the return we must receive to a return of interest and profits."

Mr. Hoover's "systematic investment of the surplus

abroad" is more in accord with the facts than Mr. McKenna's "long credits," but does it make the facts more hopeful? That our economic system, in the development of its troubles, has come to the stage at which it can make no use of much of the tribute which it collects except to set up further titles to further tribute with it, is very true; but so far from being a "remedy" for the surplus, as Mr. Hoover appears to regard it, that is an aggravation of the trouble from which the world is suffering. It increases the top-heaviness of the already insupportable load of debt from the producing system of the world to the finance of ownership, in the collection of which the whole trouble arises of the world's inability to produce what it could consume if production were related to human needs, or even to consume what little by comparison with its powers it is permitted to produce. Mr. Hoover's "remedy" is that the economics of the system should keep themselves steady by perpetually throwing themselves more out of balance and becoming more than ever top-heavy. Not being able to handle its existing surplus, ownership is to remedy that state of things by setting up claims to more surplus. It is the same sort of remedy as a man plunged up to the breast in a quagmire might achieve by floundering further in up to the neck. And, since Mr. Hoover's remedy is to keep on doing it, deeper than the neck. And then?

The Pollack Foundation of Economic Research, an institution which commands the services of a number of distinguished American economists, has dealt faithfully with all this in a criticism issued by two of its well-known members, Messrs. Catchings and Foster. They point out that

Mr. Hoover's conclusion concerning the necessity of exporting our surplus amounts to a declaration with which the business world and most of the economic world seem to agree, that there is no possible way of giving our people enough money to buy what they can readily produce. There is, he says, only one remedy, and that is by the permanent systematic investment of our surplus production in reproductive works abroad. That is to say, our money and profit economy so obstructs the flow of goods to our own people that we must regularly send abroad a substantial part of our output; and since the income of consumers abroad is also insufficient to buy our surplus, and never can become sufficient, we must permanently take our pay in foreign capital goods, in factories, mines, power-plants, and railroads. What does this mean? It seems to mean that if we work very hard we can send more wealth abroad and thus possibly receive more interest and dividends from abroad, wherewith to acquire still more capital abroad, and so on generation after generation without finding any way whereby we or our children or our children's children can ever greatly benefit by our increased productivity. According to this theory our own standard of living must remain the same as though we had never produced all this surplus wealth.

That is precisely what it does mean. Not merely what Mr. Hoover means, but what the actual facts mean. For in his description of the facts, Mr. Hoover is in the right of it; one only quarrels with him in respect of his curious view that taking payments for exports in this way is a remedy for the evil instead of being a further extension of it. Do his critics suggest that it is possible, *within our present economic system*, to "give our people enough money to buy what they can readily produce"? The system exists for no other purpose than to prevent the working mass of the people from doing anything of the sort; the purpose of restricting their permitted consumption to simple maintenance and handing over the surplus to ownership in the orthodox feudal way. For what other purpose is ownership maintained over the opportunities of the community to work and live? It is not "according to Mr. Hoover's theory," but according to the whole purpose and functioning of the economics of ownership. To "give our people enough money to buy what they could readily produce" would be to wipe out the possibility of tribute, and to substitute for the existing social order based on ownership and production for profit a new social order based on production for use. And that would mean much more than giving people the money to buy with. It would necessarily mean a social control of production and a planned output of real things to buy with the money.

Since therefore a system of production for the provision of tribute to ownership necessarily obstructs the flow of goods to the general population so as to leave an unmarketable surplus on the hands of the tribute-receiving class, all this further development of the scramble for outside markets follows in unavoidable sequence; with its incessant extension of the system until the bulk of the world's populations are brought under it and rendered incapable of consuming their own product or its equivalent by reason of having to surrender it in the tribute-payments to which all this capitalization by investments abroad is the setting up of fresh title, resulting in further surplus unmarketable within the area of the system.

The notion that this can continue in perpetuity from generation to generation is, of course, absurd. The world is wide, but it is not illimitable; and we have now reached the stage in this development at which the possibility of further expansion into outside markets, though not yet exhausted, has become inadequate in relation to the vast area of the world so developed as to be compelled to seek outlet for its volume of surplus.

A system dependent upon this sort of expansion does not come to a final stop by the complete exhaustion of outside markets. Long before any such finality is reached there is the period of closing in towards finality; a period of increasing strain and confusion; and the point of breakdown is reached under that strain.

It is through the confusions of such a period of closing in towards exhaustion that the life of the world under the present regime of ownership is now passing. The days when a few countries in which power-production was first developed had spacious access to wide world markets uncrowded by competitors have passed long ago; and the generation now living has seen the competitive struggle for the remaining outlets grow to a pitch of savage intensity, with confusion and insecurity spreading everywhere. Civilization has barely survived one devastating war incidental to this struggle. We are not yet at finality. There are still outside markets. But they have become so inadequate for the purposes of ownership driven to find outlets for the surplus unmarketable amongst the populations producing it that the scramble for them has become a fury of wild beasts, and can only be carried on through confusions that make the previous stages of the struggle seem almost placid, and with the hideous danger always present of more devastating war than ever being let loose upon the world.

The confusion during the present period of special trade and industrial depression has certainly been aggravated by sheer stupidity beyond what it need have been in the essential sequence of events by which the ownership system of the world's economy thus moves towards its own inevitable breakdown. The unwisdom with which the monetary system has been handled by the banking interests; the mere monkey-tricks which have been played with prices by the manipulation of gold and credits; the gratuitous and unnecessary reduction of agriculture to bankruptcy; all these have played their part. And by way of supreme folly in a world whose root trouble is the vast spread and constant extension of the indebtedness of the working life of mankind to the finance of ownership there has been the piling up on top of all this of the war debts; take it in all its bearings and implications the most insensate of all the follies by which the ownership government of the world has needlessly added to the load of its own inevitable distractions and confusions.

But let us be clear that these are only aggravations, accessory stupidities which could have been avoided, and not the main trouble itself. If all these unwisdoms were eliminated; if our war debts were wiped out; if our monetary system were handled with such wisdom as to stabilize prices and cut out all the mere gambling with the ups and downs of capital values and price instability, making ownership a matter of simple and sober investment; none the less the fundamental and inevitable movement of the system towards world confusion and breakdown remains as we have seen. It is on that tremendous current of the essential finance of the system itself that the affairs of the world are swept along into their present confusion; and the accessory stupidities are no more than eddies in it.

As a necessary consequence of the purposes of ownership under power-producing conditions, *the world is becoming a single area within which consuming power does not exist in proportion to output.* A single nation under such conditions, industrially developed for power-production under class ownership, would go to pieces if debarred from outside markets for its surplus; and would either have to make war to break through the ring in which it was being strangled—the world has seen such war—or change its social order so as to permit its own people to consume what they produce. If it were a small nation with small resources and a scarcity of materials, it would have to satisfy itself with a peasant life and small products. In proportion to its range and its resources it could enrich its life. But if it retained the system of ownership and tribute, it would either have to break through the ring or revert to ownership as mere peasant feudalism.

A general world industrial development for power-production under ownership-economics, becoming a single area in its common inability to consume and its need for outside markets, creates precisely the same dilemma; but on a world scale, and *with no way out* in a world itself ringed within the system. As the outside markets approach exhaustion, as they become less and less adequate, this is the problem presented to the world by the growing confusions of such a period. It is the problem of the world to-day.

The thing, surely, comes to its last delirium of unreason, its miracle of incompetence to serve the needs of human life, in this—that in a world in which everything necessary and desirable, everything that can add to the comfort and joy and fullness of human life, can be produced in greater abundance than men have ever known before, the universal exhortation to the people of the world is that we must economize, must consume less, must have our individual wages cut down and our social services reduced, so as to meet the charges fastened upon the world's life by this overwhelming indebtedness to the finance of ownership; charges of which those who receive them can make no human use, but can only reinvest them in the creation of still further charges.

CHAPTER XV

It only remains to sum up our enquiry; to see what it is the new powers are offering to human life, and what that offer means by way of new social organization for its effective acceptance.

The confusions and depressions into which the life of the world is thrown by the attempt to confine the operation of these powers within the structure of a class society as an endowment for class power and culture have created a curious illusion; the illusion that we are passing through hard times, times in which we cannot afford things. There is probably no meeting of any committee of any public authority being held anywhere in Great Britain just now at which projects large and small are not regularly turned down on the ground that, though they are wholly desirable, and indeed urgently needed in many cases, the financial position does not permit us to indulge in them; and the same consideration prevails over all our expenditure, personal and public.

The financial position, yes; that is simply a question of what is imposed upon us by the working of our system of ownership-economics. But the actual facts are another matter altogether. In the reality of things we are passing through a period of such plenty and accumulation as the world has never before known. Our whole difficulty is that it does not and cannot be got into consumption; the finance of the system forbids. What we are suffering from is "the paradox of impoverishment through plenty," as Sir Arthur Salter aptly describes it.

The phrase in common use is quite accurate, although most people who use it have not the least idea of its significance. It is not the reality of things, not the lack of resources, not the absence of plenty and to spare, that keeps us from most of the desirable and many of the urgently necessary things. It is "the financial position"; and the financial position, so far from being the inexorable law of life which most people who speak of it in that awed way apparently take it to be, is merely the distributive mechanism of the existing order displaying its incompetence to serve the world's life and obstructing the flow of the world's resources into use.

To any one who takes the finance of our present system as natural law instead of seeing it for what in fact it is, the distributive device of a social order hopelessly inadequate to cope with power-production, this contrast between the hard times of the financial position and the real facts of abundance—the contrast which is the evidence of the system's inadequacy—must be the very devil of an enigma. One catches that note of utter bewilderment in most of the references to it. "It is very extraordinary and very odd," says Mr. Lloyd George, "that we should be suffering from the overproduction of the things we all want." "The modern world," says Mr. Winston Churchill, "is suffering from the curse of plenty. Who could have thought that cheap and abundant supplies of all commodities should find the science and civilization of the world unable to use them?"

Mr. J. M. Keynes tells us how great the surplus is. "After paying wages," he says, "far higher than in France or Germany, after supporting a quarter of our employable population in idleness, after adding to the country's equipment of houses and roads and electrical plant, we still had a surplus available to be lent to foreign countries, which in 1929 was greater than the surplus for such purposes of any other country in the world, even of the United States." We must economize to the utmost limit. Why? So that a vast surplus of the wealth we produce, which we are under an inhibition neither to consume nor to exchange for other goods, may be handed over to the controllers of this "financial position" through which the inhibition operates, who can make no use of it except to establish with it further claims to the receipt from other countries of further surplus similarly unusable. The financial position is merely the measure of our almost incredible disablement under our present economic arrangements from handling and disposing of real things for the service of life.

In a word, as we have seen all through the enquiry, the system perpetually overproduces; creates a surplus, not beyond what the general life could consume if its needs were met, but beyond what it is permitted to consume by the finance of the system. That has been its constant and unavoidable characteristic. Its purpose of tribute-collection and its financial arrangements to that end compel it to distribute purchasing power insufficient to provide a market for its products.

In any sane view of life, a community producing more than sufficient for its needs would release everybody into a proportionate degree of well-earned and well-provisioned leisure. Finding itself in a position to produce on such a scale, it could and would—always presuming sanity of purpose in its social order—reduce its bondage to incessant toil for material things, and set its people free for other and higher activities. It would not be a question of an eight-hour day or a six-day week, but more probably of the six-months working year which is already the rule for University dons; or whatever less period experience might prove to be sufficient for the full and satisfying supply of all the needs of life.

The possibility of any human culture at all is dependent on such a release of men from drudgery to leisure and wealth and opportunity. When there was nothing in our methods of production to permit that release for the general life, when hard and incessant toil meant only a scanty return, nevertheless the urge of human life towards higher things than drudgery did achieve the release of a select few by the device of ownership of the community's scanty opportunities to live, and so enabled other than the drudge qualities to find some opportunity of developing in human affairs.

What power-production offers us is the general release of human life into that leisure and wealth and opportunity. And all our present trouble is in the fact that the old class ownership system still insists in the old way upon continuing to appropriate the wealth and opportunity for itself—the distributive economics of the drudge age of scanty production surviving into the new age of plenty—and breaks down under the load of surplus which it cannot consume itself and debars anybody else from consuming by its finance of tribute-collecting.

But while it continues to appropriate the wealth and opportunity for itself, it cannot appropriate all the leisure. For it is in the nature of power-production itself, and not in the defectiveness of distributive arrangements, that men are released into leisure; power-production in itself being the supersession of human labour by other non-human powers as the energy of production and measure of output.

The release into leisure takes place. Nothing can prevent that. It is the essential economic consequence of power-production. But it is a release into starved leisure, destitute and resourceless. At this moment somewhere about thirty millions of the working population of the world within the areas developed for power-production stand released in that way; and millions more in partial employment only. The International Labour Office of the League of Nations estimates at not less than a hundred millions of the world's population, men and their families, the army now suffering deprivations by unemployment; released into leisure because of the production of vast surplus wealth by non-human energies, but forbidden to use the surplus because the whole purpose of the economic system and its finance is to pass all products into the possession of the owning class in the old feudal way. The surplus has been produced for tribute and not for use in the world's life; and the finance of tribute-collection—of production for profit—does not permit it to be used for consumption unless it is first marketed for profit.

Though the problem is overproduction and getting the surplus into consumption, it must not be got into consumption except according to this profit requirement of the finance of ownership; and the distribution of the purchasing power that would put it into consumption is, in the producing accountancy of that same finance of ownership, a cost of production to be reduced to the lowest possible point.

(Do not be discouraged. The world is not really the madhouse which all this indicates. It is only a world suffering from inertia of the mind, and therefore unable so far to bring itself to question or even to see the fundamentals of a social order; these stupidities which most people have got into the petrified habit of taking for granted because they are the existing order. Courage; they *will* see.)

Our immediate way out would seem to be to distribute purchasing power and enable the release into leisure which power-production effects to be a release into provisioned leisure and an access to the unmarketable surplus. But if we distribute purchasing power by any other process than the process by which the finance of tribute-collecting distributes it, we smash the finance arrangements by which ownership carries on production. We pile up its costs of production; because distributing purchasing power means disbursing the products whose consumption is the labour cost of production. And in that way we destroy the capitalization of production; for these products consumed by labour are the capitalization of production under ownership, and there is no other reality in "capital."

Let us be quite clear about that. In the whole process of production, nothing whatever is involved but human effort applied to natural resources; in the collection of raw materials and their transport, in working them up, in making the machines and in generating the power, nothing whatever comes in or can come in at any point except human effort applied to natural resources. But human life cannot apply itself to production unless it is maintained while it works. And all the products by which human life is maintained have passed, as it is the purpose of the system to pass them, into the possession of ownership for marketing. The capitalization of production is simply the distribution to the labour so engaged of permits to consume from this stock of commodities already in the possession of ownership and on the market; the total of such permits necessary to maintain labour while it is thus employed being the capital expenditure on production. The capital itself is nothing other than the products so consumed while men are engaged in the production of further products to pass to ownership in the same way. It is what the working life of the community eats and drinks and wears and lives upon in what should be the normal course of the flow of the world's resources from the world's activities into the world's use. It appears in the finance of our ownership system as "capital," and its distribution during the course of production as "capital expenditure," because the world's resources from the world's activities do not flow into the world's use, but have been intercepted and appropriated by ownership; and "capital expenditure" is the doling of them out in maintenance allowances to the human life employed in production. It is, in short, the finance mechanism by which the purpose of ownership—the division of the flow of the world's wealth into maintenance for the workers and the surplus as tribute to ownership—is achieved.

To distribute purchasing power otherwise than by this procedure—to put the surplus into consumption amongst the millions made redundant by power-production—would, therefore, in the degree in which it enabled the surplus to be eaten up, smash the basis on which production is carried on under ownership. For all such consumption is a cost of production in the finance of the ownership system; whether such rights of consumption are distributed in actual wages, or by public funds raised by taxation to effect its distribution outside the wages system, or by printing paper money and issuing it as legal tender, or in any other imaginable way. Whatever the form of it may be, any distributed right to consume means that ownership has to part with the financial value of the product so consumed. In brief, its "capital" disappears; for as we have seen, its capital is nothing but the product on which the world lives.

In parting with it by payment of wages, ownership does not lose it; because that is a payment made in the course of further production replacing the consumed product. But in parting with it by any of these other forms of distribution, the "capital" of ownership vanishes into consumption with no replacement to the owner; and the finance of production is smashed up by unproductive costs which leave no surplus, no tribute, no profit accruing to ownership in return.

A simple distribution of purchasing power by itself is, therefore, obviously not the way out. No really adequate distribution of purchasing power is possible within a social structure in which production is governed by this finance of ownership. The attempt to distribute adequately brings production to a standstill by destroying the finance of its capitalization. And it is this reaction upon production itself of any consumption to which the right has not been distributed through the finance of further production for ownership profit that creates and explains the mystery of the "financial position" in which a community finds itself unable to consume in the midst of abundance.[1]

[1] Note, too, that this reaction upon production takes place even when the consumption is in the course of further production if that further production is outside the finance of ownership. The nation, for example, or a local authority may distribute consuming rights in wages to men employed in, say, the production of new roads or other public equipment. But that is production outside the finance of ownership. It is carried on by the taxation of ownership—that is, by taking from ownership the financial

It is upon this method of production that the world depends for any sustenance at all within the existing social structure. It is the only exercise of our power of production permitted by the finance of the system. So that even the thin sustenance allowed to the working life of the community is menaced if we attempt to make it any greater by these other methods of distribution. Ownership points out, with quite unanswerable logic as against such proposals, that they all mean increasing the costs of production to the point of unprofitableness; and that with such unprofitableness production is checked and employment decreased. We should, if we attempted to extend such a policy of simple distribution without regard to its effect upon production, find ourselves with nothing left to distribute; for we should be destroying the finance requirements of the system for carrying on production itself. Always assuming that we leave the conditions and the control of production itself as they are, this is final checkmate to any merely distributory way out of our difficulties; the way of any social reform which accepts the present finance of production as the basis of things.

For its continuance at all, ownership has to demand from the working life of the world an acceptance of poverty as a condition of being employed at all; lower

value of all the consumption of the workers engaged—and the product does not pass to ownership for toll-collecting, which would be the form of marketing and price recovery of values in the case of roads. Although there is a real utility product, the money spent in it therefore counts as unproductive costs in the finance of ownership, and the "financial position" is accordingly drawn as tightly as possible against it.

wages or no work; reduced costs of production—that is, less claim by the working life of the community on the products of the world's work—or no production. And to that demand, which is in itself so incompatible with all the implications of a new age of abundance as to be an abdication of reason from human affairs, there is no answer whatever to be given once we accept the ownership and control of the world's producing activities for private profit as the governing principle of social organization. The consequences in distribution follow automatically; they are those "inexorable and inevitable laws of political economy" of which we hear so sternly whenever we blaspheme against the inhumanities of the system; the laws by which, once you assume the system itself to be inevitable, its consequences in human life follow inevitably. As they do.

* * * * *

And with that we get to the essential conflict between the economics of ownership and the implications of power-production in human life.

What the new powers offer to us is the release of the general life into leisure and wealth and opportunity; and that release must mean a distribution of our abundance into general consumption; a distribution which as we see the whole procedure of the system works to render impossible, under menace of the collapse of production itself if it is attempted.

There is only one conclusion from all this. It follows with clear certainty that such a distribution can only be made through a new social control of production, planned for use and consumption according to the world's needs. That is the way out, and there is no other.

* * * * *

This release of the general life of the world into leisure and wealth and opportunity is as unavoidable in the consequences of power-production as our present distresses are unavoidably the consequences of attempting to deal with the abundance of power-production within a feudal social structure. The release into leisure is effected in any case, for that is in the unavoidable immediate consequences of power-production; in its essential character, indeed, rather than its consequences. But the release into wealth and opportunity is a distributive arrangement subject to obstruction by human folly and lack of understanding; and the achievement of it may be made a long-drawn-out agony of maladjustment in human affairs. If it is so obstructed, it can, as in the case of all nonadjustment of life to new conditions, only be to an accompaniment of confusion and discomfort in human affairs, growing in intensity the longer the obstruction persists, and threatening a disruption of civilization if the adjustment is too long delayed.

The strains and tensions of this incompatibility between the purposes of ownership and the implications of power-production, the warnings of impending disaster, are manifest everywhere. In the inability of the world to consume or ownership to market the surplus of power-production through distributive processes expressly designed to prevent the passing of the world's resources into the general life, with all the accompanying social conflicts, business confusions, and international de-civilization of human relationships, is there any one of us who can fail to see the evidence of the breakdown of feudalism as a possible principle of social organization under the new life-conditions for mankind brought about by power-production?

If the analysis of our troubles here made is sound in fact and substance—and I believe it to be incontrovertible—what we are face to face with to-day is the exhaustion of the possibilities of carrying on with the feudal principle of social organization in a world in which the basic conditions of human living have been changed by the coming of the new powers. It is the deepest and most fundamental change in history. It has revolutionized the whole character of the struggle of man with nature for sustenance; transforming man's part in it from drudgery to mastery and his reward from sparse living to a splendid abundance. And the task to which we have to set ourselves is nothing less than the creation of a new social order for making effective this release of mankind into the new age of general available plenty which the new life-conditions offer us.

The basis of such a new social order can be no other than the social control of production, planned for use and consumption in the general life up to the level of human needs. Within no other social order than such a social control of production for human service implies, superseding the old feudal control for profit, can the economic consequences of power-production be contained. The disruption of any narrower social system seeking to contain them for narrower class purposes is now so manifest in the affairs of the world that nothing but a miracle of blindness and mental inertia can permit men and nations to drift further towards it. With the form which our social and political activities may take in the conscious and intelligent effort towards the new order, it is no part of my task here to speak. I am concerned only with defining the purpose of the effort; and that purpose, if the world is to avoid final disaster by the breakdown of a visibly disrupting social system into chaos, can be no other than the purpose of the Co-operative Commonwealth.